ISLE OF MAN
CHURCHES
CHAPELS
AND KEEILLS
EXPLORED
IN
WORDS
PICTURES
AND MUSIC

Churches of Mann

Lily Publications Ltd
PO Box 33, Ramsey, Isle of Man,
British Isles IM99 4LP

Tel: +44 (0) 1624 898446 Fax: +44 (0) 1624 898449
Website: www.lilypublications.co.uk
e-mail: sales@lilypublications.co.uk

AUTHOR: JONATHAN KEWLEY
ORGANIST: GARETH MOORE
PHOTOGRAPHERS: MILES COWSILL & VICKY HARROP

INTRODUCTION

BY JONATHAN KEWLEY

As the mist clears and the sun breaks through, a mountain clad in purple heather sweeps down to the western sea; on the rocky shore, seals bask; overhead, gulls cry and choughs swoop. Halfway up the slope, on a bracken-covered ledge, are the ruins of a small stone building. It is a chapel, old already when the last of the Viking Kings died. In it, a priest murmured the ancient words of the mass and venerated Patrick and Columba, the saints of the Celtic west. Every few years, a packhorse made its way down the narrow path, bearing on its back a body to be buried in this holy spot. Long after the last priest had joined his saints, the final funeral trudged this way, while at the same time across the seas in France, a Queen was pulled to the scaffold and the modern age began.

Just a few miles away over the hills, the evening sun shines through a window and lights a neat whitewashed church. Its interior brings to life the maxim of the old High Tories, 'Every man in his place, and a place for every man'. Sunday after Sunday its people made their way to their own little enclosure of panelled wood where, secure in their position, they looked out over the sea of their neighbours, old and young, rich and poor, and settled down to hear their black-gowned parson preach Parliament-approved doctrine, that by Faith alone was the way to salvation and another life. And the window through which the sun came – it is full of angels, in the right hand of each a drawn sword, in the left a shield bearing the cross of St George, the martial saint who was patron to the greatest empire the world had seen, and not least patron to a dead Major in the Bombay Staff Corps who, after years in the stifling heat of Aden, had ended his days on this cool and windy Island. He was the husband of a daughter of one of its most ancient families, who had raised the window to his memory.

These two spots, the first Lag-ny-Keeilley at the end of the road south from Dalby, the second Malew Church, a mile north out of Castletown, symbolise between them the contrasts and the continuities which are the history of Christianity in the Isle of Man – Celtic and English, Catholic and Protestant, proud and humble, flourishing and desolate – and which shape, too, the story of its buildings, those churches and chapels which dot the Island and which are the subject of this book.

It is in three sections. First I will endeavour to trace that story and to describe the buildings and what is significant about them, with the aid of some of the splendid photographs Miles Cowsill and Vicky Harrop have taken as part of a project to picture every one. Then, in the main section, more of these photographs, chosen by Miles as his personal selection, speak for themselves. Finally Peter Jones, whom the Island is lucky to have as its resident organ-builder, gives his expert view of some of the best organs, which, on the CD which accompanies the book, are played by Gareth Moore, that incomparable ambassador for Manx church music.

The book aims to be a readable introduction to the subject. It is hoped that a further, more detailed volume, will follow, and that will contain the references the present format does not allow. Information will also be available on Lily Publications' website www.lilypublications.co.uk.

Any mysteries of ecclesiastical or architectural terminology not explained in the text will, I hope, be solved by the short Glossary which begins on page 166.

Thanks are due to Miles Cowsill and Vicky Harrop for all the photographs; they in turn would like to thank the guardians of the various churches and chapels who allowed them access, and also Helen Hyde who helped in so many ways. Thanks, too, to Gareth Moore and Peter Jones for the music side, and to Charles Guard for his assistance here; to Wendy Thirkettle and all the staff at the Manx Museum Library for their unfailing help and patience, as always; to Frances Coakley, whose website A Manx Notebook (www.manxnotebook.com) is an unparalleled source of material on all things Manx, and in this context, particularly on all things Methodist; to the staff of Lambeth Palace Library; and, most of all, as without it this book would not have appeared, to the Manx Heritage Foundation for its financial assistance.

CONTENTS

CHURCHES OF MANN

© Lily Publications 2009
© Text: Jonathan Kewley
© Photographs: Miles Cowsill and Vicky Harrop
Published by Lily Publications Ltd
Produced and designed by Lily Publications Ltd
Printed in Italy

MANX CHURCH BUILDINGS

THE BEGINNINGS

Tradition has it that Christianity was brought to the Isle of Man by St Patrick in the fifth century, at a time when Roman rule in what is now England was breaking down. It is quite possible that he or missionaries sent by him visited the Island which is clearly visible from his base in Co Down, but equally evangelisers may have come from Whithorn in Galloway, again within sight of Mann, where St Ninian had founded a monastery the century before. In any event, the Island was Christian some time before St Augustine arrived in Canterbury and began to convert the English.

The Manx people at this date were Celts, a race divided into two branches, one of which later became the Irish and the Scots, and the other the Welsh and Cornish (having been driven west by the invading Anglo-Saxons). Both branches seem to have been represented on the Island at the time.

There are no written records to tell us how the conversion of Mann took place, but it is likely that rulers were converted first and then adopted the new religion on behalf of their people. Christian burial places grew up, served by priests who received the burial fees. They will have built themselves small chapels and huts at each site, the same structure perhaps doing duty as both. The first of these may have been of mud and turf; in any event, they were replaced by stone buildings, the foundations of a number of which survive.

They are what are called field churches, scattered about the countryside (there were then no towns); in the Island, twentieth-century usage has been to call them 'keeils', which in fact simply means 'churches' in Manx. They were small, on average perhaps 16' by 10'; they were presumably used primarily by the priest to say mass, and it is uncertain to what extent they saw any sort of congregational worship. They do seem to have been a focus for burials, and most have graveyards attached.

There is some controversy as to how many there originally were. The evidence from place-names is that there were certainly more than survive today. It has been suggested that there may have been one for each of the land divisions called treens (the size of four large farms), but this is unproven. It is

Previous pages: St Michael's Chapel, Fort Island.
Above: Lag-ny-Keilley.

The east keeil at Maughold. The round structure at the back right is a later well.

also uncertain how many (if any) date from the first centuries of Manx Christianity, which lasted until the Viking raiders started to colonise the Island about 900, and how many are later; the Norsemen, who had their own religion, converted to Christianity within a generation or two.

None of these field churches survives as more than low ruins. St Michael's Chapel on Fort Island gives an idea of what they were like, although quite a bit larger; it (and they) would have been thatched. At Maughold, on a headland at the north-east tip of the Island, there seems to have been a Celtic monastery; there are defensive earthworks and the heavily-restored remains of at least three chapels. St Patrick's Isle, now the site of Peel Castle, may also have been a monastery, with its eleventh-century round tower like those at Irish monastic sites.

THE STRUCTURE OF THE CHURCH

In the twelfth century, as part of a process changing church organisation throughout western Europe, the Island was divided into seventeen parishes, with one church designated as the parish church, which all inhabitants were supposed to attend every Sunday. Given the size of the new parishes (perhaps twenty times the average in parts of lowland England), it is unlikely they did, unless spurred by prosecutions in the Church Courts.

Up until the late eighteenth century, Church and State were intertwined in a way difficult to understand today. Everyone was subject to the Church in the same way they were subject to the government of the King or Lord, and the two powers usually worked together. The Church had its own Courts which dealt mainly with moral lapses (they determined how much maintenance the father of an illegitimate child had to pay right up until 1924); the parish was one of the main units of local government, the parson acting in conjunction with the churchwardens who were elected and directed by the Vestry, the assembly of ratepayers; they dealt, and could levy rates to pay for, not only the repair of the church, but also roads and what we would today call social security.

The parson was called rector in Andreas, Ballaugh and Bride, vicar elsewhere. This was not just terminology. The value of 'livings', in other words how much the minister received to live on from the various available sources of income, varied substantially, but the rectors were much better off than the vicars. In the mid- nineteenth century (when some evening-out had already taken place) the Rector of Andreas received £807 a year but the Vicar of Marown only £150. This explains, incidentally, why some clergymen moved from one parish to another on what today seem downward career moves, but actually made sound financial sense.

7

The crypt of the Cathedral.

Herringbone masonry in St Patrick's.

The rectories were reserved for the most important of the clergy – the Archdeacon at Andreas (down to 1978) and the Vicars-General at Ballaugh and Bride. The latter were the judges of the Church Courts, but unlike today, when there is only one who is always a lawyer, up until the early nineteenth century there were two who were clergymen.

The Archdeacon was (and still is) Archdeacon of Man, while the Bishop, the head of the Church of England on the Island, is Bishop of Sodor and Man. Sodor is a hangover from the days when the Norse Kingdom of Mann and the Isles included what we now call the Western Isles but which (if you were a Viking looking from Norway) were the southern isles or Sudreyjar, whence 'Sodor'.

The Bishop is a feudal baron of the Isle of Man (the only one surviving) and as such has a seat in the Tynwald Court, the Manx national assembly; at one time he received rents or taxes from the inhabitants of his barony which was principally in parts of Braddan, German, Jurby, Marown and Patrick, as well as around his palace at Bishopscourt, between Michael and Ballaugh. Originating as square 'pele tower' like those on the Scottish borders, it seems to have been begun in the thirteenth century, and remained the residence of the Bishops continuously until 1974.

THE FIRST PARISH CHURCHES

The churches chosen as parish churches may sometimes have been picked because they were in a convenient location, but in other cases it must have been because of their special sanctity or some other reason, as they are far from central; Lonan Old Church is the supreme example, right at the very southernmost corner of the parish. Some may already have been big enough for their new role; old St Patrick's, in Peel Castle, has 'herringbone' masonry from the tenth or eleventh centuries (so contemporary with Saxon work in England).

Little remains of these first parish churches, which have been patched, extended and rebuilt over the centuries, although Maughold Church contains a few fragments in the Romanesque style which are unlikely to be later than 1200. The greatest amount of mediaeval fabric survives in Malew Church, Lonan Old Church and the Old Grammar School in Castletown, which was a chapel. They were typically a simple stone rectangle, with a bellcote at one end. Although never a parish church, the roofless St Trinian's Chapel in Marown gives the best impression of what they looked like.

St Cecilia's, Jurby.

The only mediaeval church building of any elaboration was the Cathedral, in a supremely picturesque position rising sheer from the rocks on St Patrick's Isle at the mouth of the River Neb. In total contrast to the stark simplicity of the parish churches, it shows the full panoply of the Gothic style universal in England at the time. It is cross-shaped, with pointed stone arches under the central tower dividing chancel, nave and north and south transepts. More arches separate the nave from a south aisle which has since disappeared, and under the chancel is a stone-vaulted crypt used as the ecclesiastical prison. The earliest part of the Cathedral is the east end, from the early thirteenth century, with typical Early English lancet windows. The growth of Peel Castle around it made it a tempting quarry for materials for military works, and by the seventeenth century much was in ruins. Projects to restore it have come to nothing.

It is likely that other churches had some mediaeval Gothic stonework, but apart from some windows at Maughold Church and a window and piscina at the fourteenth-century St Cecilia's Chapel, Jurby, all that survive are disembodied and re-used fragments. The most ambitious early feature is the arcade at the Old Grammar School in Castletown, the Island's ancient capital. The division into parishes took no account of towns (then non-existent or at least unimportant), but as they grew, places of worship were provided in the form of chapels of ease, of lower status than the parish church, but a convenient alternative for normal weekly services. The only one which survives today is this one at Castletown, extended and converted into a school in the late seventeenth century. The date of the arcade itself is the subject of some dispute, anywhere from the thirteenth to the sixteenth century. It is handsome work of St Bee's sandstone from Cumberland.

One possibility is that it came from Rushen Abbey at Ballasalla. This was the Island's principal monastery, founded in 1134. It was comprehensively demolished (and the materials sold off) at the Reformation, but a tower and a few subsidiary buildings survive; excavations are ongoing. Nothing is now visible of the only convent on the Island, the Priory of Douglas which gave its name to the Nunnery, a country house now occupied by the Isle of Man Business School; the so-called Nunnery Chapel is Victorian. The third religious house was Bemaccan Friary, established by followers of St Francis of Assisi at Ballabeg; the chapel has been preserved by subsequent use as a barn.

Virtually nothing survives of the interiors of the Manx mediaeval churches, but the more important at least would have had carved woodwork, wall paintings and stained glass. At Malew Church there is a small piece of wood from about 1500; it has one of the earliest carved representations of the three legs of Mann.

Above: The Round Tower on St Patrick's Isle.
Overleaf: St Trinian's.

THE REFORMATION

The Reformation was a slow process in the Island, as in many of the remoter parts of northern England, but by the beginning of the seventeenth century it was Protestant, and a recognisably-Anglican Church held sway. The parish churches were still very simple structures with windows small and few in number, and so they would have been dark inside. During the late seventeenth and early eighteenth centuries many were modernised or rebuilt, and one of the most noticeable features are the large, round-headed windows. These were filled with clear glass (as at, for instance, Old Kirk Braddan today) to give good light, especially as increasing literacy meant people would read their prayerbooks, not just repeat the responses after the parish clerk.

Some churches were extended to cope with a growing population, and the opportunity could be taken to add a fashionable bell-turret at the west end, as at Ballaugh Old Church. In contemporary England, full-scale church towers were a sign of the superiority of the Church of England over 'Dissenters' whose chapels had no tower or bell. In the Isle of

Man, which was nearly 100% Anglican, that consideration did not arise, and it may have been thought unnecessary to go to the expense of a proper tower, a feature which, by the end of the eighteenth century existed only on the Cathedral and at Michael, Braddan and the new St George's.

Sometimes extension was not enough. Arbory, Rushen and Santan churches were completely rebuilt, allegedly because the old structure was defective, but also from a desire for a fashionable new church. They were on more or less the same sites as their predecessors; Patrick and Lonan were rebuilt on new sites more convenient for the parishioners. Extensions and repairs of varying extent took place at many other churches, notably Old Kirk Braddan (where a tower was added) and Malew.

The period also saw improved church provision in the growing towns, with chapels of ease rebuilt in Castletown, Douglas and, later, Ramsey; St Peter's in Peel was used as the parish church because the actual parish church was the often-inaccessible Cathedral.

THE AUDITORY CHURCH

Before the Reformation, the interiors of the churches were arranged to suit Roman liturgical practice; the congregation did not need to hear the priest intoning 'the murmur of the mass', which was anyway in Latin. They were dark, the light reduced by small windows, probably of stained glass, and the chancel where the priest officiated was cut off from the people in the nave by a wooden rood screen (there is a fragment of what may be one at Malew Church).

After the Reformation, the Protestant doctrine of the Church of England meant that the people needed to be able to hear the parson preaching and reading the service (which in the country was often in Manx well into the nineteenth century). In consequence they were arranged as 'auditory' (or hearing) churches, with everyone facing the parson in his (usually-combined) desk and pulpit, a good example of which survives in Old Kirk Braddan. Seats at the east end of a church, near the altar, faced not it, but the pulpit. Communion services (which did use the altar) took place usually only four times a year.

If more space was needed, it made more sense to build on a wing at right angles to the existing building in an L or T shape, with seats facing the parson at the centre, than to extend at one end where it would be more difficult to hear or see. On the same principle, most churches ended up with galleries, again bringing people as close as possible to the parson. Seating, both in the galleries and at ground level, could be raked like in a theatre. In a prominent place were the Royal Arms, symbolising the position of the Church of England as the established church, subordinate to Crown and Parliament.

These auditory churches were full of light, with plain glass in the windows. Walls were whitewashed, and the pews were grained to look like oak, or sometimes painted brown. There are a number of good Georgian church interiors in the Island,

Previous pages: The old Cathedral.
Above: Old Kirk Braddan.
Right: The west front of Ballaugh Old Church.

Previous pages: St Mark's.

Above: The T-shaped Malew Church; everyone faces the parson, the slope of whose desk can be seen on the right, just to the left of the organ.

precious survivals of so many later destroyed by the Victorians. What is important is not so much any one feature but the whole ensemble, filling every part of the building with box pews, each with its own door. By law, everyone was supposed to go to church, and so provision had to be made for them (whether they did in fact go or not). In the parish churches pews were allocated to each farm, and in the towns they could be sold or rented to provide an income. Most at least of the upper and middle classes very much wanted their own pew, as to sit with the poor in seats at the back would seem to them to invert the natural order of things. In Castletown they went as far as clubbing together to pay for an extension to Malew Church to accommodate pews for themselves. Such private pews can perhaps be seen as the equivalent of a season ticket today at a football ground or at the theatre or opera.

Records are not always clear who was the moving force behind churchbuilding in the seventeenth and eighteenth centuries. It may have been concerned parishioners, but equally many resisted because they knew they would have to pay through the (compulsory) church rates. Often it was at the instigation of the bishop; both Thomas Wilson (bishop for no fewer than fifty-seven years from 1698-1755) and his successor Mark Hildesley (in post until 1772) promoted what one might call better facilities for worship; the new chapel at St Mark's built in 1772 was named after the latter.

Many English churches from the mid-seventeenth century onwards were in the classical style, exemplified by Wren's City churches or James Gibbs' St Martin-in-the-Fields. In the Isle of Man, only the west fronts betrayed any classical influence in the eighteenth century, with pilasters at Ballaugh Old Church and bell-turrets on Rushen, St Mark's and Santan, among others. The only classical interior was St George's, Douglas, deliberately upmarket and modelled on St James', Whitehaven, which would have been familiar to merchants and other travellers. Some more classical features appear by the Regency, notably Venetian windows at Jurby Church and St Paul's, Ramsey. These two share a certain 'look' with some other churches of the period such as Michael Old Church, whitewashed with red sandstone quoins and other dressings, reminiscent of Cumberland or south-west Scotland. They also have towers, which become more popular at this time, conceivably to differentiate the churches from the Methodist Chapels which were springing up from the 1770's onwards.

METHODISM

Apart from a few families of Quakers in Maughold and a few low-key Roman Catholic merchants, neither of whom had any special place of worship, the whole population of the Isle of Man were Anglicans until the arrival of John Wesley, the founder of that more evangelical variant of Anglicanism called Methodism. He remained a clergyman of the Church of England to the day of his death, and his followers continued at first to go to church (i.e Anglican) in the morning and chapel (i.e. Methodist) in the evening. Even today, the distinction is

Leodest Chapel.

less clear-cut on the Island than elsewhere, with some Methodists still thinking it only right to have their funerals in the parish church.

Through the nineteenth and much of the twentieth century, the Church of England and the Methodists dominated religious life on the Island, each claiming the adherence of half or so of the population. The two denominations were referred to as Church and Chapel, and Anglicans spoke of 'going to church' and Methodists as 'going to chapel'. Historically, a church means a parish church, and everything else, Anglican or Methodist, was a chapel; the 'Church' places of worship in Douglas and Castletown were always called 'Douglas Chapel' or 'St Mary's Chapel', and strictly they became churches only when made separate parishes in 1879 and 1921, respectively. However, by then, not only had many Anglican non parish churches become known as churches in popular speech (because they belonged to 'the Church'), but the Methodists had started to refer to their larger structures as churches too. Today, other than in legal documents, all buildings of whatever denomination tend to be referred to as churches except the small, rural Methodist chapels, which retain the name with some pride in their history.

The first Methodist chapels were very modest, and domestic in scale ; they often had ordinary Georgian sash windows. They continued to be built in rural areas well into the nineteenth century; the best surviving example is Leodest in Andreas; others include the old chapel at the Cooil and that

(now a house) at the Garey. They were small, taking only a few dozen people, and scattered widely throughout the Island. Their interiors were like those of contemporary churches, whitewashed and with box pews; that at Leodest is especially fine.

Numbers grew rapidly until the Island was 'half Church, half Chapel'. Larger, more ambitious buildings were needed, such as the Wesleyan Chapel in Arbory Street in the then-capital, Castletown in 1801 (now the Schoolroom); it was galleried and church-like in scale. A decade later, Kerrowkeil ,a few miles away in the hills, copied the 'churchy' look on a

Above: The old Primitive Methodist Chapel in Castletown, now the Masonic Hall.

Overleaf: Old Kirk Braddan, with the three-decker pulpit on the right.

The former chapel at the Garey.

smaller scale.

By the 1820's Methodism had split; the majority (mainly middle class) stayed as 'respectable' Wesleyan Methodists, but many working men were attracted to the Primitive Methodists, initially nicknamed Ranters. The new denomination soon had its own chapels throughout the Island, too. The larger ones are distinctive in being two-storey, with a hall on the ground floor and the chapel itself above. A very early example of this is what is now the Masonic Hall in Hope Street, Castletown, with all the windows entirely domestic.

GOTHICK

Roman Catholics were growing in numbers and confidence as legal restrictions on them were removed in England and Ireland. There were still some anti-papal riots and so they thought it prudent to build their first chapels on the outskirts of the towns, for example at the Green (then really a separate village near Castletown) in 1828; it is a simple building without a tower, the original interior probably very like an Anglican church; a Gothick gallery survives.

The Gothic style had never entirely died out in England, but most eighteenth century essays were 'Gothick', light-heated and playful with pinnacles and arches used as decoration on a structure which was often largely classical in shape. The best example on the Island was St Mary's in Castletown, rebuilt in 1825 for use not only by the inhabitants of the then-capital but also by the government and the garrison in the Castle. It is symmetrical, as a classical building should be, but has Gothick detail applied – the arch above the door, label mouldings over the windows, an octagonal lantern (taken down in 1912) on the tower, and a Gothick frieze to the (now-destroyed) gallery-fronts. The principal windows have Gothick tracery – the typical Georgian glazing bars curve and intersect as they come to the point at the top; examples can also be seen at the Roman Catholic church in Castletown. Battlements were another Gothick feature, especially dominant

at Crosby Chapel and perhaps redolent of the church militant; many mediaeval churches did have them, of course.

This period marked the emergence for the first time on the Island of professional architects, something which was happening through provincial Britain as well. The earlier churches had been designed by their builders in conjunction with the clergy and local gentry. The process is not clear-cut, however; some of the earlier builders (for instance Thomas Quayle at Arbory Church, rebuilt in the 1750's) were men of some design ability, and the first architects were often builders as well – the change was as much one in the social status of the architect as any other change of role.

George Steuart, who worked on the Island up until his death in 1806 and designed the Castle Mona, the Duke of Atholl's fine new mansion overlooking Douglas bay, produced a church of some distinction at Shrewsbury (the circular St Chad's), but no ecclesiastical building on the Island other than the great obelisk in Braddan churchyard to Lord Henry Murray. The next generation is represented by two near-contemporaries, John Taggart (c 1777 – 1836) and Thomas Brine (c 1767-1840). The former, a Manxman, designed Jurby Church in 1812 and a number of now-demolished Methodist chapels; the latter, who had come to the Island on government business but married a Manx girl and set up in practice, was the architect of St Paul's, Ramsey (started in 1814 and owing

St Mary's, Castletown.

Above: St James', Dalby.
Overleaf: St Luke's, Baldwin.

much to Jurby) and of St Mary's, Castletown. He did a lot of work restoring Castle Rushen, the well-preserved mediaeval castle in the centre of the old capital; he was probably responsible for adding the little bell-cote on the former St Catherine's Chapel high on the ramparts.

THE WARD CHURCHES

After Waterloo Lord Liverpool's government was anxious to ensure that there were sufficient churches for a transformed, industrialised country, and so a mass church-building programme ensued; the results are called Commissioners' or Waterloo Churches in England, and First Fruits in Ireland. The Manx equivalent are those built or rebuilt under the energetic episcopate of William Ward, who as a result of somewhat sycophantic adherence to the family of Prime Minister Goderich was Bishop from 1828-1838.

By this time, a Gothic style was seen as more 'suitable' for churches, and this was a more serious manifestation than its Georgian predecessor, although it still did not intend to create facsimiles of mediaeval buildings. It sometimes looked further back into the Middle Ages, with long, narrow lancet windows ubiquitous, but also liked the light and graceful Perpendicular Gothic of the fifteenth century. Most of these new churches were cruciform, and generally had a separate chancel or sanctuary because theological changes were making the clergy

see the altar as more important. Modern technology was not eschewed, however, and many have iron galleries and windows.

Ward raised the money by a public appeal in England, and the well-known drawings of the Manx churches as then existing are a relic of this; one wonders if they were in fact all as dilapidated as portrayed. The amount collected was not huge, and all the new churches had to be built for much less than most of the Commissioners' churches in England, and so inevitably there had to be some skimping on detail. Later in the nineteenth century, they went totally out of fashion but are now at last being appreciated in their own right for what they are. Many are actually rather good, with picturesque silhouettes and spacious, light interiors, especially when decorated as originally intended, as at Michael and St Jude's, both recently triumphantly restored. On a smaller scale were some chapels of ease built to counter Methodist influence in the remoter parts of some parishes; Dalby, where the western hills look to the setting sun, is especially good, half chapel, half schoolroom, and pinnacles all over.

The interiors of the Ward churches are simple and practical, often with two aisles for ease of access rather than one in the centre. They are sometimes, as at Michael, more classical than Gothic. There is usually either a gallery, or provision for one if the population grew. In fact in many rural

Left: Lonan New Church.
Above: Michael Church.

areas it fell shortly after they were built, but there were always
a large number of empty pews at ground level, because the
practice of allocating them to particular farms took no account
of landowners who were Methodists or just non-churchgoers.

Ward, who was suspicious of many of the Manx,
encouraged parishes to use new architects from England, the
Welch brothers, the elder of whom was a partner in the firm
which had the contract (which bankrupted them) to design
the vast new town hall at Birmingham – a building which
bears no resemblance whatsoever to what they did on the
Island. Taggart designed one of the Ward churches (Lonan) as
his plan was cheaper and the Vestry (the paying ratepayers)
insisted; Brine does not seem to have been approached.

SERIOUS GOTHIC

The style of the Ward Churches survived into the second
half of the century at the Dalrymple Memorial Chapel at
Union Mills. Church architecture nationally, however, was
getting more serious under the influence of the Oxford
Movement and the Ecclesiologists, a pressure group who
wanted the Church of England to return to pre-Reformation
practices and to copy their ideal mediaeval churches, inside and
out. St Thomas', Douglas, of 1847 is still not far removed from
a Ward church, and the first real leaning towards the new ideas
on the Island is St John's. Designed by the Manchester

architect Richard Lane in 1849, it is the setting every year for
part of the annual Tynwald ceremony where recently-enacted
laws are read to the people. Its spire dominates the area, and
indeed rather overawes the Tynwald Hill itself.

Over the succeeding half-century, heavy, 'archaeologically-
correct' Victorian churches sprang up all over the Island, in
response to an urbanising population, liturgical change and the
growth of non-Anglican denominations. There are no
masterpieces, and only two are by an architect of the first rank
– New Kirk Braddan and St Matthew's, Douglas, both by John
Loughborough Pearson, the architect of Truro Cathedral (he
had Manx family connections). St Olave's, built as a chapel of
ease for growing North Ramsey and designed by a London
architect, Michael Manning, is one of the best.

Others are pedestrian, such as Thomas Barry's large church
at Peel, initially a white elephant as Peel people preferred their
existing place of worship, but finally made the parish church
and, in 1980, as its founders had hoped, a new cathedral for
the Island. After the old cathedral lost the last of its roof,
national services and the enthronements of new bishops were
held at St Mary's, Castletown in the nineteenth century and St
George's, Douglas in the twentieth, although officially the 'pro-
cathedral' was the private chapel at Bishopscourt, added by the
London architect W.G. Habershon in 1858.

Many of the smaller Victorian churches were mass-produced designs by that most prolific of church architects, Ewan Christian (of Manx descent); Marown New Church is typical of his work. His cousin, John Henry Christian, who worked with him, could produce more original designs, and the rebuilt Bride church is an example of how successful a modest Victorian village church can be. Christ Church the Dhoon is interesting in being not Gothic but Romanesque (neo-Norman) with windows and doors round-headed, not pointed; the effect is one of great solidity.

There were, however, grievous losses over the period, notably the early eighteenth-century old St Matthew's in Douglas (perhaps the building on the Island most frequently painted by artists, standing picturesquely behind the town market). Both Ballaugh Old Church and Marown Old Church were truncated by the demolition of their eastern (and older) half after the erection of a successor.

The interiors are generally much darker than their predecessors', with much stained glass (added as funds or donations allowed), carved woodwork and candles amid the 'dim religious light'. Above all they focussed resolutely on the altar, itself ever more elaborate, which came to be seen as central to their services. Nothing could block the view of it from the main doors, and it was raised up on steps, to increase its status. It remained the holy of holies in the Sanctuary at the very east end of the church, separated from the people by stalls for clergy and that new innovation, the robed choir. The people themselves sat in or knelt at open benches, the Ecclesiologists seeing box 'pues' as the proper habitat of independent Protestant Georgians, not devout ritualist Victorians.

Even some quite new churches were altered to fit this pattern; the most elaborate scheme of decoration is that of St Thomas', Douglas, where a rood screen partitions off the chancel and the walls were painted all over with remarkable murals by the Manx artist John Millar Nicholson.

But while Anglican architecture sought to recreate the churches of the Middle Ages, when England had been catholic, Roman Catholic architecture of the period did not, and must be understood on its own terms. Just as the Reformation introduced auditory churches to concentrate on Protestant sermons and readings, so the Catholic Counter-Reformation, the Jesuits to the fore, emphasised preaching; all their congregations, too, had to be able to hear the priest. The architects of Roman Catholic churches were therefore told (especially in the Liverpool Archdiocese to which the Isle of Man belonged) that their models should be not mediaeval parish churches with crossings, screens and separate chancels, but the spatial construction of the Continental Baroque – even if clothed in Gothic dress. St Mary of the Isle, the Island's main Roman Catholic Church, is a good example of this – and it explains why it feels very different from Anglican churches of the same period.

The desire among Anglican architects to use 'correct' Gothic meant that anything else had to be purged. The 'restoration' of an old church, allegedly in disrepair, gave them their opportunity, and hundreds of English churches were ruined in this way, the accretions of centuries scoured and scraped, to be replaced by dead, often mass-produced features. As Betjeman wrote:

> 'The Church's restoration in 1883
> Has left for contemplation
> Not what there used to be...'

The Isle of Man did not escape. Most grievously affected was Maughold, an ancient building when Queen Victoria came to the throne but now largely the work of her reign. The eastern (roofed) half of Lonan Old Church is now smothered with Victorian cement. Georgian buildings suffered, too, the attempt to graft Victorian Gothic onto a classical core of an entirely different style producing the unfortunate results visible today at St George's, Douglas, St Paul's, Ramsey and Arbory Church, with classical proportions and architectural features married to pitch pine benches, stained glass and shiny, mock-mediaeval encaustic tiles.

CLASSICISM

It would be wrong, however, to think that all church-building on the Island after the 1820's was Gothic; there was still a strong classical tradition among the Methodists, to whom indeed Gothic was suspect as redolent of High Church, even popish tendencies. The greatest of these buildings, now demolished, was Victoria Street Chapel in Douglas, its main façade by the very competent local architect John Robinson. The best of those surviving in use are Glen Maye and Michael, both from the 1860's but, especially the former, looking earlier. Others include Waterloo Road in Ramsey (distinctly Italianate), Atholl Street in Peel, and (most elaborate of all, with its giant fluted Doric columns, even if now converted to secular use) Glen Road in Laxey. The Island is fortunate in still having this important collection.

Gradually Methodists accepted some Gothic features, which came to be seen as no more than a sign of a religious building. They also grew in confidence as they became clearly a separate denomination, with strong political influence. Rebuilding to provide more space often produced a new chapel with some Gothic features alongside an earlier classical or simply domestic one, kept on as a Sunday school; a good example is at the Cooil in Braddan.

As early as the 1830's larger new chapels in Castletown and Port St Mary were Gothic at least to the extent of being bedecked with pinnacles and having pointed windows; the

The Centenary Methodist Chapel of 1839 in Atholl Street, Peel.

latter (now demolished) was a copy of King's College Chapel, Cambridge, substantially simplified and on a rather smaller scale. The larger town or village chapels of the end of the nineteenth century tended to be fully Gothic. Commentators since have tended to see 'Nonconformist Gothic' as the lowest abasement of that style, although there are now the beginnings of a reappraisal. Its apogee on the Island is Rosemount, built in 1886 to serve the prosperous, influential and socially-confident Wesleyan Methodists of Upper Douglas, and known only partly-jocularly as the Methodist cathedral.

INTO THE TWENTIETH CENTURY

By 1900 taste was moving away from serious, vertically-emphatic Gothic to something less formal and with more horizontal stress. The influence of the Arts and Crafts movement made large roofs a prominent feature. An early Manx example is Mount Tabor Chapel, Port St Mary, of 1903 by Southport architects Todd and Morris. Within the next decade came Park View Chapel, Michael, by the local architect Joseph Teare, and St Ninian's, Douglas, a large church by W D Caroë, with, until recent regrettable alterations, an interior of noble simplicity.

The masterpiece, however, is Our Lady Star of the Sea and St Maughold, the Roman Catholic Church in Ramsey, designed by Giles Gilbert Scott, architect of Liverpool (Anglican) cathedral and built in 1909. It is a tall, light-filled single space, with a much lower baptistery off to the north, all lined in a greyish brick; the use of colour for the fittings is exquisite.

During the nineteenth century a large number of ancient stone memorials were discovered, some in churchyards, others built into later buildings. Most are now thought to date from the early days of Viking rule on the Island. They have been called crosses although some do not bear that symbol and most are rectangular rather than cross-shaped. The categorisation of these by the Manx archaeologist (and later first curator of the Manx Museum) P M C Kermode, and the publication of his work, led to a realisation they needed to be properly displayed. The local Arts and Crafts architect Armitage Rigby designed cross shelters at two of the churches with the largest collections, Michael (where it forms a lychgate) and Maughold.

On the Continent, this was the era of Art Nouveau or the Jugendstil. Little percolated to the Island, although some of the windows of Sulby Methodist Chapel (by Teare, 1914) show Art Nouveau influence. The chapel and crematorium in the Douglas Borough Cemetery can best be described as Eclectic meets Moorish.

The large stock of existing places of worship meant there were few new ones in the inter-war years, and in fact disposals of surplus buildings began after the Wesleyan and Primitive

Left: Mount Tabor, Port St Mary.
Above: Detail from the west doors at Jurby Church.

Methodists merged in 1932 (although many remained separate congregations into the 1970's). Some Anglican churches were altered to cater for more Anglo-Catholic sensibilities, for example the fine woodwork by Kelly Bros of Kirk Michael in a number of churches, notably the screen at Onchan.

The great masterpiece of 1930's Modern on the Island is the reordering of Jurby Church by Wilfred Quayle, an interesting local architect, in 1939-40. The tower was reduced in height and topped with a shallow pyramidal cap of Italian inspiration. A brown brick north porch was added, and the rainwater goods all renewed in aluminium with figures of St Patrick and decorative mouldings. Inside, what had become essentially a Victorian interior was cleared out and replaced with clean modern fittings The colour scheme is cream walls with a pale blue and turquoise ceiling. The doors incorporate panes of partly abstract stained glass comparable to some of John Piper's work.

MODERN TIMES

After the War, official vandalism saw the gutting of St Mary's, Castletown, and the demolition of Victoria Street Chapel and St Barnabas' in Douglas and of most of St Peter's in Peel. The fightback began only with a group of public-spirited individuals who formed the Friends of St Jude's to

Close Rhennie Chapel.

stop the closure and demolition of one of the Ward churches on the northern plain. They were successful and have restored it to a high standard. However legal protection in the form of designation as listed buildings (in the Island called registration) is far from complete.

During the 1960's both the Church of England and the Roman Catholic Church changed much of their liturgy so that their Eucharistic service (Communion or the Mass) was celebrated by the priest standing behind the altar, facing the people, rather than the other way round. This necessitated the reordering of many churches. Sometimes the existing altar was simply move out a few feet, but in a number of cases a new 'nave altar' was installed, with varying degrees of success. It was perhaps easier in churches of auditory (i.e rectangular) plan, such as St Mary of the Isle; some others, such as St George's and the new cathedral, may not yet be in their final form. Often kitchens or lavatories have been added and pews removed to make more space (though sometimes with their ghost left as a patch of floor awkwardly different from the aisles). The most serious damage through reordering is the two-storey structure inserted at the west end of St Ninian's, turning an impressive long interior into an oddly-proportioned square one.

Other churches have survived but in other uses. The greatest number are former Methodist chapels, redundant not only because of the amalgamation of the two denominations

into one, but also because rural depopulation destroyed the base for so many small rural chapels. Most have been converted, with varying degrees of sensitivity, into houses, workshops or offices. Non-domestic use often allows the windows to remain full-height and the chapel-shape to stay recognisable; a good example is Close Rhennie Chapel, deep in that patchwork of wet woodland and small meadows called the Ballaugh Curraghs, and still intact except for a large new door at the back, invisible from the road. The smaller and more domestic in scale, the easier conversion usually is.

The Anglican chapels-of-ease built by the Victorians have

St Joseph's, Willaston.

There has been some good repair and redecoration of churches, notably Michael and St Mark's, as well as St Jude's. New churches have been few in number and often domestic in scale, the intention being that low, horizontal buildings are friendlier than awe-inspiring tall ones; St Joseph's, Willaston, from 1957, looks back to the Arts and Crafts tradition, while St Anthony's, Onchan, from the 1980's, is more overtly modern, with a remarkable interior seemingly wider than long. The more recent Baptist Church in Port St Mary is more traditional in shape, no doubt copying the massing of the Methodist chapel which stood on the site, but perhaps also reflecting the confidence of a new and numerous congregation.

Head and shoulders above other ecclesiastical buildings of the post-War years is All Saints', Alexander Drive, Douglas, fitted into a late-Victorian suburban site by local architect Claude Kneen in 1967. It clearly owes much to Our Lady Star of the Sea, but is in an altogether more modern idiom, with structural steel and concrete. The interior includes interesting modern glazing and woodwork, all of a piece, and lightweight metal screens.

SOME THEMES...

STONE

The older churches are all built of local stone, the nearest available, quarried near the site or brought from the shore. Over most of the Island, this was what used to be called slate but is now more properly 'Manx series'. There is a grey limestone in the south, at Castletown, Ballasalla and Port St Mary, red (and a very little yellow) sandstone at Peel in the west, and a dirty-cream granite from south of Foxdale in the centre. The Manx series itself varies markedly in colour from mid-grey through distinctly brown to almost black. A non-traditional effect can be achieved with modern cutting methods, as at St Ninian's. At St Anthony's it is no more than cladding.

Peel sandstone is the only freestone (stone which could be carved and so used for windows and arches), but it is very soft and weathers badly. Only two churches are built entirely of it (Old Kirk Patrick and St Peter's, Peel). Later, red sandstones were imported from England, to be used first for quoins at the corners (such as St Paul's, Ramsey) and later for more extensive decorative work as at St Olave's, Ramsey and St Matthew's, Douglas. Other Victorian imports include Bath stone as dressings at New Kirk Braddan.

Local granite was used for quoins at Bride, for the tower at St Mark's and for the bell-cote at Marown New Church. The only church built entirely from it is St John's. Most Castletown limestone has been rendered over and so is not visible, except on St Mary's-on-the-Harbour in Castletown. The variant

All Saints', Alexander Drive, Douglas.

also been vulnerable to declining populations. Derbyhaven and Cronk-y-Voddey have both been converted into houses but retain their bell-cotes and so continue to make a contribution in the landscape. The former Primitive Methodist chapel in Malew Street, Castletown, a tall, grey-stone building with a slate-covered spirelet, is built at the top of ground rising up from the inner harbour. It is now offices but, almost completely unchanged externally, it, too, remains the focus of vistas within the town and from the surrounding countryside. In Douglas, the Scottish Kirk on the corner of Finch Road and Prospect Hill, opposite the Legislative Buildings (the 'wedding-cake') and so perhaps the most prominent position in town, was demolished and replaced by a nondescript commercial office block, but the planners insisted on the retention of the spire which thus remains part of the panorama of the capital. The congregation moved to a former Girl Guides' headquarters, a building entirely unecclesiastical in character.

Two former schools, both of architectural merit, were given new leases of life as churches. The fine, pedimented Mathematical School in Peel, dating from the 1840's, became the Elim Pentecostal Church, while in Castletown, the old National School of 1838 metamorphosised into St Mary's on the Harbour, a refuge for the Anglican congregation made homeless by the closure of old St Mary's.

The chancel of the old Cathedral showing the sandstone used for the windows, original stone on the left, later restoration on the right.

called Pooilvaaish marble, which is black when polished, is not suitable for building but has been used for paving, and clads an interior wall at All Saints', Alexander Drive.

Brick is a rarely-used material in the Island, although some of the earlier Methodist chapels in the north (where there is no available stone) are built of it, and it is used in the interior of New Kirk Braddan and on the exterior of the Red Cross Hall in Douglas (originally a chapel of a small sect, the Methodist New Connexion).

Traditional stone building used lime mortar, but later pointing has sometimes been in cement (there is particularly hideous raised ribbon pointing at Onchan), potentially harmful to the stone. Like Manx cottages and farmhouses, the older churches were often whitewashed inside and out, and extra protection against salt gales was achieved with a lime render. From the early nineteenth century this was replaced by cement, which prevents a building 'breathing'. The twentieth century contributed pebbledash, as at both Maughold and Arbory. Now conservation directives are seeing a return to lime.

ROOFS AND TOWERS

The only old tower is on the old Cathedral, but the eighteenth century saw most churches get a small tower or turret (perhaps a better word as they are solid, not hollow) with one or two bells, usually capped with a cupola or little dome. The nineteenth century had huge ambitions for not only proper towers, but spires on top, but many were either never built or blown down – including New Kirk Braddan, the present Cathedral, St Matthew's and St Thomas'. Those which were built and survive include Lezayre (perhaps the most picturesque), St John's, the Scottish Kirk in Douglas (now attached to a modern office block) and the Dalrymple Memorial Chapel at Union Mills. Towers without spires might be finished with battlements (as, rather primitively, at St George's), with a pitched roof (as at St Mary of the Isle, where the towers are unfinished) or what is called a Saxon helm (as at St Peter's).

Bride Church, showing the contrast between the red sandstone door surround, the granite quoins, and the dark Manx series stone used for the walls.

Above: The Old Grammar School, Castletown. Below: One of the unfinished towers of St Mary's of the Isle, Douglas.

None contains an ancient peal of bells, although more modern rings exist at St George's and the new Cathedral.

Except possibly for the Old Grammar School there are no old church roofs on the Island, all having been re-roofed over the years. The first non-thatched roofs will have used Manx slate, but it does not split well, and imported slates were preferred, traditionally graded, so the smallest were in the top row and the largest at the bottom. There is in fact a great uniformity in the slate roofs of Manx churches; there is no lead or copper, and tiles are rare (most spectacularly used at Our Lady Star of the Sea, where they light up the exterior).

Most eighteenth or early nineteenth century churches and chapels had ceilings, which were an important part of the design; they survive at Old Kirk Braddan and in most of the Ward churches. There is often an ornamental ventilator to the roof space. Some ceilings have been removed to accord with later fashion, which was for open, timber ceilings, often of some complexity. They are usually dark, at least until the installation of modern lighting. The better twentieth century architects made features of the ceilings of their churches, and Our Lady Star of the Sea, Jurby and All Saints each have fine examples.

INTERIORS

The Island has some important Georgian church interiors. Good box pews survive at Old Kirk Braddan, Malew, Leodest,

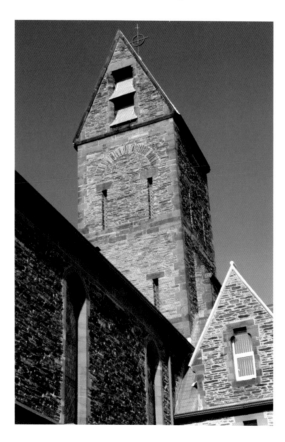

Above: St Stephen's, Dalby. The pews have lost their doors.
Right: Bride Church, a typical Victorian rural interior.

Dalby, Michael Methodist Chapel, Michael Church, St Jude's and Santan. They are called box pews because they are square or rectangular in shape, with doors completely enclosing them. Those in the chancels of Braddan and Malew have the most varied shape. Originally each landowner would have erected his own pew, but gradually uniformity of height and design was introduced, and in fact most of the Manx boxes are nineteenth century. They are usually made of deal, grained to look like oak (as at Malew) or painted brown (as at Braddan).

The survival of other components of the Georgian interior is more sporadic. Braddan has a complete three-decker pulpit (the parish clerk, who led the congregation, sat in the bottom tier, and the parson in the middle; he preached from the top). As the parson always read the lesson himself, there was no need for a separate lectern. Braddan also has its eighteenth-century altar rails (like a contemporary staircase), and those at Malew are being restored, to surround a very unusual feature for the Island, a stone altar from St Mary's in Castletown dating from 1704. Generally 'holy tables' (the correct Church of England name) were wooden, just like domestic tables, as they are officially supposed to be movable. Near them were usually wooden boards with wording from the Communion service – the Creed, the Ten Commandments and the Lord's Prayer, useful for those who did not possess their own prayerbooks (they were not generally handed out in churches until the twentieth century).

Other notable features include hat pegs at Marown Old

Church, and upholstered seating in what is perhaps the grandest family pew, the North Gallery at Malew. The fashion for open benches rather than box pews was slow to take hold on the Island, and a number of mid-nineteenth century seatings are effectively benches with very low doors at the end, such as St Thomas', Marown, Arbory and Rushen.

The Georgian churches were all of a piece, in uniform colours and materials; walls were white, woodwork brown, glass clear. Victorian church interiors could be as cluttered as a Victorian drawing room. Pulpits became very ornate, and were often of stone; that at St John's has a special staircase leading through the wall to it. Altar rails became low and open, and often went the full width of the church, leaving the altar in sacred isolation where a century before several pews would have been fitted in. Altars developed embroidered frontals and bore book-stands, candlesticks and crosses (the latter previously totally taboo in a Protestant church; they were thought to imply Catholic idolatry, kneeling before a crucifix).

Because the Church of England in the Island had generally been 'Low', and so quite resistant to Anglo-Catholicism, some changes came later than elsewhere, and in many cases not until into the twentieth century (and later in Methodist chapels than in Anglican churches). The catalyst for change would often be the arrival of a new parson who expected everything to be as it was in his previous parish across; a new Vicar of Malew in 1919 was scandalised to find the churchwardens counting the collection on the altar and soon gave directions

for the offerings to process in front of him to the vestry in a seemly manner.

For the first time since the Reformation it became permissible for an Anglican church to have more than one altar, and Lady Chapels (usually for small-scale weekday services) were created at St George's and Lezayre. These then needed carved screens to separate them off, and rood screens dividing the choir and clergy in the chancel from the people in the nave were erected in a number of places including St Thomas', Onchan and St Olave's. Much of the carving of these was by the firm of Kelly Bros in Michael. There was a tendency to use oak rather than grained deal, which should be longer-lasting but could clash with older woodwork, something which became far worse in the later twentieth century, as at Santan where the fine, very dark box pews and gallery are confronted with undistinguished light-wood chancel furniture, which it is to be hoped can one day be replaced.

Methodist interiors generally followed Church of England precedent, although with a much greater tendency to have a central pulpit, generally behind the altar (unlike in a few Anglican churches, like St Mary's, Castletown, where the pulpit was directly in front).

As we have seen, galleries were the preferred means by which the capacity of an auditory church could be increased. Some we can date. The front at Arbory is probably from the 1760's, with fine panelling, and the North Gallery at Malew was put up in 1818. At St Mary's, Castletown, there were for a time some galleries at second-floor as well as first-floor level.

In many English churches, and no doubt in Mann, too, the west gallery provided a home for the small orchestra of instrumentalists who accompanied the services. A singers' pew, for an early (and definitely unrobed) choir tended to be near the parish clerk, who led the singing. When organs first came into use in the Island in the mid nineteenth century, a number were housed in west galleries. This had the advantage of not taking up space at ground level (a difficulty in the older churches without transepts to tuck one away in), but it did mean the loss of the gallery as sitting space. A selection of Manx organs is described in more detail in the Appendix. From a visual point of view, the most noteworthy are at Sulby Methodist Church, where the central part of the case is good Georgian work, and at St Thomas', very elaborately carved with a looseness heralding Art Nouveau.

WINDOWS

The most sudden change to the appearance of our church interiors came with Victorian stained glass. When Queen Victoria came to the throne in 1837, every Manx church or chapel window was clear glass; by her death in 1901, probably a majority of windows in Anglican churches were filled with coloured glass, entirely altering the interior effect.

The reason why the Church of England had abandoned stained glass at the Reformation was that, with its subjects generally saints, it was seen as encouraging the worship of these saints as petty divinities, rather than reserving all adoration for God alone. Wall paintings and statues were proscribed for the same reason. As a result, attempts to reintroduce it were viewed with some suspicion, and early examples can generally be identified with High Churchmen of the Oxford Movement. The first in the Island was the east window at Malew Church in 1842 by William Wailes, a well-

Above: The porch window at Andreas Church.
Right: The east window at Malew Church.

known glass-maker in Newcastle who had been patronised by Pugin, the arch-mediaevalist and designer of the interiors of the Houses of Parliament.

The secret of how stained glass had been made in the Middle Ages had been lost, and so the first attempts were not very good; the colours were weak and too bright, and the glass itself was thin. In design, however, they tried to replicate mediaeval examples, often figures on panels set against a geometric pattern, looking overall rather like an oriental carpet; the Malew east window is a good example of this.

Later the technique was rediscovered, and colours became stronger, although this sometimes made the windows very dark. By the turn of the century, grisaille work, in silvery grey, was sometimes included, as it had been in the Middle Ages, to lighten the effect.

Typical Victorian stained glass can be seen in many of the Gothic churches of the era, the design consisting often of quite static figures imprisoned between the stone mullions and tracery. Where windows were inserted in the round-headed windows of the Georgian churches, however, the artist had freer reign to make a composition, and the most successful can be reminiscent of painted glass of the eighteenth century; one of the best examples is the Poulsom window at Malew by a Liverpool firm, Jones & Willis.

Many of the principal firms of stained glass manufacturers and designers are represented on the Island, including Lavers and Westlake (Malew) and Clayton and Bell (New Kirk Braddan). The well-known Glasgow glass artist Daniel Cottier made a fine window at Lezayre in memory of his parents, with figures of saints on panels on a background of small panes of clear glass, each bearing a golden flower. A firm with Manx roots were the Kaylls of Leeds, who there produced glass almost exclusively for Roman Catholic churches, but on the Island worked for Anglicans, too; at St Mark's the east window is theirs (and is the only stained glass window in the church – very much the effect in most churches in the early phases, where the window above the altar would be coloured first). As everywhere, however, the majority of windows on the Island are unsigned and so accurate attribution can be impossible.

Not all window glass was figurative. The east window at Lezayre, given by the squarson in memory of his parents in the 1850's, is entirely patterned in a gorgeous lattice of red, blue, gold and silver, perhaps at that date in deference to potential opposition. Methodists were generally unable to accept the images of saints in their windows, but did develop an enthusiasm for patterns, often in pastel tones as at Arbory Street Chapel in Castletown.

The Art Nouveau glass at Sulby Methodist Chapel has already been mentioned; the long, horizontal window in the porch at Andreas is also worthy of note, just rectangles of green and circles of red, bullseye panes between. The greatest twentieth-century glass on the Island, however, is the two windows by the Irish artist Harry Clarke in the Roman Catholic Church in Castletown, seemingly out of a Celtic fairy tale with each colour in a multiplicity of shades. Running it a close section are the doors at Jurby, again already mentioned. Other significant modern glass is the window, also at Jurby, by Joseph Nuttgens, and several at Bride and St Olave's by the distinguished maker John Hayward. The element in modern taste which prefers a monochrome palate is catered for by the etched glass window at St Anthony's, Onchan, by local artist Christopher Spittall, which preserves the view of Douglas Bay and hence shows Christ apparently walking on the water.

Every bit as important historically as the stained glass windows in Manx churches are some of the late Georgian iron windows. Most are filled with clear glass, the ironwork forming a lattice pattern within Y-shaped tracery. There are a number in the Ward churches which look original, notably at Michael with (later?) coloured glass at the edges of the frames. Of similar date are the tall windows in the entrance front of Arbory Street Chapel, Castletown. Other examples are at St Mark's, Orrisdale Chapel and Quayle's Hall.

MONUMENTS

Before the Reformation, those wishing to commemorate a relative who had died would pay a priest to say masses to assist the passage of the soul through Purgatory to Heaven. Once this had become illegal, the practice grew up of erecting a monument in a church instead. The Island does not possess anything to compare with the elaborate Elizabethan and Jacobean monuments which are the glory of many English parish churches; the only memorial from the sixteenth century is a very scrappy stone with nothing more than a short inscription (at Malew). A century later, the monument to Christian Norris on the ruins of Michael Old Church is a primitive imitation of a classical monument with a rectangular tablet beneath a triangular pediment.

Considerably more sophistication is shown in the monument in Malew Church to a student, Julius Caesar †1735, a plain tablet of local stone with a pediment-topped surround of wood painted to look like marble. Contemporary is the striking monument in Marown Old Church to Henry Clucas †1732 ; the angel looks out with an enigmatic stare from underneath a Georgian male hairstyle, and in fact is comparable to some representations of the 'winged soul' in gravestone art.

By the third quarter of the eighteenth century marble, ubiquitous in England or Ireland, was being used for Manx monuments, too. Very few are signed, but they were almost certainly carved off the Island, with the lettering sometimes being added on arrival. Notable examples are the draped urn

H.M.S. Victory on Captain Quilliam's monument at Arbory Church.

Bryan Kneale's Illiam Dhone at Malew Church.

(more drapery than urn) to Dorothy Taubman †1784 at Malew, excellent columns to Richard Ambrose Stevenson †1773 at Arbory and, rather later but in the same church, a representation on an urn of the stern of H.M.S. Victory; the memorial is to Capt. John Quilliam †1829 who steered her at Trafalgar. The only representation of the deceased at this period is of the controversial banker (and mortgage forecloser) Edward Gawne †1837 in Rushen Church, side-face in white marble relief.

The artistic quality of marble memorials declined as the nineteenth century went on, and in fact largely died out under High Church pressure to use a stained glass window or a brass as a memorial instead. The latter are generally undistinguished,

an exception being the chequer-bordered brass to Governor Raglan †1921 at Onchan by the Liberty's metalwork designer Archibald Knox. After the Great War the Anglican authorities endeavoured to persuade families to abandon any sort of memorial and instead give an object in memory of the departed; this may initially have been useful in supplying, free of charge, the extra crosses, candlesticks, etc, which more ritualistic churchmanship demanded, but it resulted in the dreadful clutter of second-rate objects to which so many churches have degenerated (salvation, from a visual point of view, comes in England with redundancy and vesting in the Churches Conservation Trust, who are ruthless in consigning such impedimenta to scrapheap or auction, to the inestimable

The angel on Henry Clucas' monument at Marown Old Church.

The font at Our Lady Star of the Sea and St Maughold.

benefit of their buildings).

There is, however, one outstanding modern monument, that unveiled in Malew Church in 2006 in memory of Illiam Dhone (Brown William), a controversial but important figure in seventeenth-century Manx history. It is in the form of a bust by the Manx sculptor Bryan Kneale R.A.

FONTS

Christian doctrine traditionally made baptism a precondition for eternal life, and so fonts at which it could take place were an important feature of mediaeval churches. In the seventeenth and eighteenth centuries there was a tendency to use small, movable basins instead, but the Oxford Movement wanted theological importance to be matched by physical mass, and so mediaeval fonts were retrieved from churchyards or new ones created in all the mix of granites and marbles only the Victorians could devise. There are no carved fonts on the Island from the Middle Ages. There are a number of granite bowls which have at some stage been installed in churches as fonts, but whether they were created as such or were actually large mortars is debatable. There are good examples at Malew (with a nineteenth-century stem) and at Marown Old Church (two, built into the wall).

The Victorian fonts are generally undistinguished, but there are three twentieth-century examples of some quality. The first in date is at Our Lady Star of the Sea, a drum of hammered metal wreathed in fruitful vines. Next comes Jurby, of cream stone with an elaborate lid with blue wrought iron scrollwork embracing a gold cross. The third is at All Saints', Alexander

Drive, also in stone, octagonal and tapering down to the ground; the ring-chain design on one panel attests to the growth in interest in a (sometimes mythical) Celtic and Viking past. A font with great panache is the carved wooden one at St Fingan's, Glen Auldyn, the bowl supported on the tails of two heraldic dolphins.

FLOORS

The earliest field churches and their parochial successors had earth floors. Later, stone or brick paving was introduced, often disturbed by burials. It was customary for at least the higher-status parishioners to be interred underneath their pew, or sometimes in the central aisle. Spots near the altar were especially favoured (as when Governor Greenhalgh was buried by the altar at Malew in 1651). Where the burial was in a visible spot (not hidden under a pew) it might be covered with a ledgerstone, usually of dark stone with a carved inscription. Examples survive at Old Kirk Braddan and Malew. They are always laid so as to be read when standing with one's back to the altar, because then the stone is the same way as the body which (as with outside burials) was always placed so that when resurrected, according to Christian doctrine, by the sounding of the Last Trump, it would be able to stand straight up facing east (to Jerusalem and the risen Christ), and not have embarrassingly to scrabble round looking for its Saviour

Bishop Wilson objected to burials within churches, and from his time each new church built was subject to a ban on the practice. Ledgerstones thus dried up as a means of paving the aisle, and so plain stone was used instead. The Ecclesiologists looked to the Middle Ages for inspiration for an alternative, and found it in the encaustic tiles, terracotta-coloured or polychromatic, which had paved many mediaeval churches (examples have been found at Rushen Abbey). Unfortunately their copies were often mass-produced, shiny and over-bright. They can be effective in Gothic buildings but jar badly in Georgian ones such as St George's or Arbory; in England modern practice is generally to replace them with more suitable stone, although that has not been done on the Island. A good example of the appropriate use of encaustic tiles on the Island is at St John's Church where there are elaborate designs in the chancel with the symbols of the four evangelists.

Wood was used especially for the platforms on which box pews were constructed, or as a floor surface under pews at ground level. These are attractive and now often have the patina of age, from which modern cleaning and polyurethane varnishes need to be rigorously excluded if an overemphatic shininess is to be avoided. During the second half of the twentieth century many church floors were covered with fitted carpet (which can if done well be effective, as at St Mark's); the twenty-first century is gradually removing them, partly for aesthetic reasons, partly as a result of fashion in domestic

Ledgerstones at Old Kirk Braddan.

interiors, and perhaps partly because more effective heating makes the warm look of carpet less psychologically important.

CHURCHYARDS

Most burials were not, of course, inside a church but in the churchyard surrounding it. All the ancient parish churches had their own graveyard. Some seem originally to have been round or oval in form which suggests that they may be older than even the first parish church. Jurby churchyard contains what is believed to be a Viking tumulus, perhaps a pagan burial.

Up until the end of the seventeenth century people were buried without any headstone, and so the same plot could, after a while, be used again. Even then it is likely there were established burial areas within the yards for different families. The first stones lay flat and were primitive copies of ledgerstones; a number are still in situ outside Lonan Old Church. The full story of the development of grave monuments is outside the scope of this book, but headstones were near-universal by the end of the eighteenth century, and as the plots could not be re-used, yards started to run out of space. Extensions were made (one of the earliest at Malew in 1827), and later two of the largest parishes created on fresh sites what were cemeteries in all but name, at Braddan in 1848] and German (which includes Peel) in 1853. Both had their own small chapels for on-site funerals. A municipal cemetery was established in Douglas in 1899 but otherwise the parish churchyards have always been used for the burial of

parishioners of all denominations and none; for many years Patrick churchyard contained the graves of Mahometan Turks who had died in the internment camp at Knockaloe in the Great War; they were repatriated in the 1970's.

Not all Anglican chapels-of-ease had their own churchyard; the lure of the mother-church was strong, as was the lure to the parson of burial fees which he would not want to surrender to the chaplain of the new establishment. St Mark's, St Jude's, Baldwin and Foxdale have them, Dalby, Sulby and the Dhoon do not. In the towns, St Mary's, Castletown never had a yard (the rock probably rather near the surface anyway) and (old) St Matthew's, Douglas had lost its by the eighteenth century (the marketplace, now the Legion Hall, marks the site). The Victorian and Edwardian town and village churches are uniformly without graveyards.

The only non-Anglican burial places were the Rhullick-ny-Quakeryn, the atmospheric hill-top resting place of the persecuted Maughold Quakers in the decades either side of 1700, and a small, enclosed yard behind Peel (Wesleyan) Methodist chapel in Atholl Street, opened in desperation when the parish churchyard filled up. Some Roman Catholics were in Georgian days interred on Fort Island in the vicinity of St Michael's chapel (whose pre-Reformation consecration made it holy ground for them).

Each of the old churchyards has its own character due to the materials used for its gravestones. In the south, Castletown limestone was used almost universally, the effect a uniform pale

The Presbytery (on the right) at Our Lady Star of the Sea and St Maughold.

The Hall at Christ Church The Dhoon.

grey. On the northern plain at the foot of the hills, splittable slate was available and therefore provided the older graves. In the east, imported red sandstone is dominant. This last gained ground everywhere as the nineteenth century wore on, only to be edged out by white marble and black and, later, grey granite; the more recent sections of the churchyards are therefore much less distinctive.

The greatest change of the last half century has been the general abandonment of the kerb which surrounded the grave plot from the early nineteenth century onwards, and the introduction of lawn graves, all grass except for the headstone itself. This was a noble idea, influenced by the immaculate cemeteries of the Imperial War Graves Commission, but alas reality intrudes in the shape of garish materials, flower vases and the determination by the authorities to pack as many plots in as possible, saving on path space by having the stones back-to-back, not in uniform rows facing the same way as war graves do. Fortunately the Island has largely escaped the official philistinism which in some places in England has removed headstones to create an easily-mowable expanse of grass; the only two instances are at St Peter's, Peel (where many have been preserved, although not in their original positions) and at Ballure, the original chapel-of-ease for Ramsey, which was sold off as a house in 2005 ; the gravestones have been laid on the ground and public access to them preserved.

Many of the kerbs were originally the bases for iron railings which very determinedly set the plot aside for private burial. The style of the ironwork mirrors that of railings in front of contemporary town houses – from tall, straight railings in the eighteenth century to elaborate cast-iron scrollwork by the end of the nineteenth. Many were removed during the second world war on the (erroneous) pretext that they could be melted down for the war effort; families were generally allowed to opt out, and for a time at least one churchyard kept its gates locked at all hours to prevent the scrap men entering.

The best survivals are at Marown Old Church.

THE SETTING

The church or chapel, with or without a churchyard, may be the centre of the composition, but is not the whole picture. Surrounding it will be the various dependent structures which have grown up over the centuries. There will be a stone hut for the sexton who looks after the churchyard (even, at Lezayre, a house). There will, if it is an Anglican church, be a house for the minister, called a rectory, a vicarage or, if there was only a chaplain (and as a generic term), a parsonage. These reflected the status of the parson; Andreas Rectory, residence of the second highest ecclesiastical dignitary, with his own seat in Tynwald, was a substantial house even in the later seventeenth century. The old Rectory at Ballaugh, by the Old Church, was a very desirable dwelling in the mid eighteenth century. In other, less well-endowed parishes there were frequent complaints about the tumbledown state of the parsonage or even, as at Malew and Marown, that it had tumbled right down and disappeared altogether.

The early nineteenth century saw not only the beginnings of an improvement in clerical incomes, but also a campaign to build worthy residences for Victorian gentlemen-parsons with large families and often several servants. Of these, Rushen Vicarage of 1839 makes a most attractive composition right next to the church. Others were on sites some way from the church, as at Braddan. Many parsonages were sold off during the twentieth century to be replaced by smaller, less imposing dwellings for a less confident clergy; at the time of writing the only historic parsonages still in church use are Bride Rectory and Onchan and Patrick Vicarages, with the last under threat of sale.

Methodist manses are merely houses for the minister, rarely next to the chapel or purpose-built; in any event, Methodist ministers serve a circuit with many chapels and usually live in

Maughold Churchyard

the principal town. The Roman Catholics, in contrast, with an unmarried clergy, prefer their priest to live next to his church, and the Presbytery, as the residence is called, is frequently part of the church complex. At St Mary's of the Isle it is the most obviously-visible part, making up (rather grimly) much of the Prospect Hill frontage. At Our Lady Star of the Sea it is distinctly domestic (and definitely Arts and Crafts) but the tall gables echo the dominating vertical of the tower.

The growth during the nineteenth century of Church and Chapel organisations such as the Mothers' Union and Sunday schools raised a demand for a church or chapel hall, fostered, too, by an increasing seriousness in religion which shrank from the use of a place of worship for secular purposes. A more relaxed attitude in recent years has seen some sold off (prompted, too, by the cost of maintaining two large buildings). Churches or chapels in towns or villages were more likely to have halls than those in the country, partly because there was more scope for community activities but perhaps also because the tradition of using a rural parish church for many purposes died hard; meetings of the Vestry, the assembly of ratepayers which governed the parish, were held in the parish church until in the 1890's the loss of most of their powers and the abolition of church rates ended widespread attendance.

The grandest hall is perhaps St George's in Douglas, with three floors; it is now let as a wine bar and offices, having also had an incarnation as a courthouse. Running it a close second is the hall built for Peel Methodist Church in Atholl Street and

now the Centenary Centre, an arts venue; a visitor looking at the exteriors when it was in Methodist ownership might have had difficulty in deciding which was the chapel and which the hall. Rosemount is an example where the hall and other ancillary rooms were integrated into a unified complex.

Architecturally by far the most important church hall on the Island is that at Onchan, some way from the church, designed by the Arts and Crafts architect M H Baillie Scott who spent some of his early professional life there. It is very simple but with a pagoda-like fleche on top of a steep slate roof, and prominent chimneys. The hall at Christ Church the Dhoon is an interesting example of inter-war design, the walls a mixture of stone and roughcast, the roof of green slate with dormers and upswept eaves, and above the entrance a window directly below a very attractive chimney.

TO CONCLUDE...

Churches resonate with people in different ways. To a clergyman, they are a workplace; to church-crawlers, they are the country's great free art gallery. The devout worshipper genuflects, not seeing the anthropologist studying him from behind the pillar. They are in any case the most easily accessible of historic buildings, and most repay a visit, whether in person, or through the pictures which follow.

This page and right: St Matthew's Church on the North Quay, Douglas, the centre of Manx Anglo-Catholicism, built 1895-1908 to the designs of J L Pearson, architect of Truro Cathedral.

The monument to the Revd Philip Moore, an eighteenth century chaplain, (left, upper middle) came from the previous church.

The east window (right) is by William Morris & Co, the firm founded by the great socialist designer and author. The magnificent carved and painted reredos below it dates from 1916.

This page and left: St Mary of the Isle, the principal Roman Catholic Church on the Island ('the Isle' is Conister Rock in Douglas Bay, (which has the Tower of Refuge on it), sometimes called St Mary's Isle). It was designed by Henry Clutton and opened in 1859. Its height and general spaciousness meet the design brief of Liverpool Archdiocese at the time; all the congregation could see and hear.

Top left and top right: The high altar was designed by Giles Gilbert Scott, the architect of Liverpool (Anglican) Cathedral and designer of red telephone boxes.

Top Right, middle left and above: Rosemount Methodist Church (now officially called Trinity), built on a very prominent site at the main crossroads in upper Douglas from 1886 onwards. The interior is typical of a large Methodist town chapel, with galleries, two aisles rather than one in the centre, and a pulpit above the altar. Dominating everything is the organ.

Top left: Pulrose Methodist Church, erected in 1928 on a new housing estate built for those displaced from central Douglas by slum clearance. It is classical, with a pediment and round-headed windows, but the detail is unmistakably of its own time - a rare example of inter-war classicism on the Island

Top left and top right: All Saints', Alexander Drive, Douglas, the best church built on the Island since the Second World War. It was designed by a local architect, Claude Kneen, and consecrated in 1967.

Bottom right: St George's, Douglas, was started in 1761, and the interior, with its classical columns and galleries, is based on St James' Church at Whitehaven in Cumberland (then the main port for travel to and from the Island). It has sadly been much altered since, but this view shows something of the original intention.

Middle left: The bells at St George's.

St George's Church, Douglas.

The classical design was subverted by Victorian alterations such as the new pews and encaustic tiles (above). Edwardian work was more sympathetic to the original, even if veering more to the Baroque, such as the splendid cover (top right) to the now-disused font. Stained glass windows were fitted in the Georgian openings; this one (middle left) commemorates the naval captain son of a former chaplain of St George's.

Right: The exterior, like the interior, was modelled on St James', Whitehaven, although there the tower has good classical detailing rather than the Douglas church's rudimentary (and cheaper) battlements.

Right: This spire is all that remains of the Scottish Kirk of 1867 by the local architect John Robinson, who designed many of the best buildings of mid-Victorian Douglas; on the left are the Legislative Buildings, also by Robinson.

Top right: ITop right: Inside St Andrew's United Reformed Church, a former Girl Guides headquarters next door to St Ninian's in upper Douglas. It serves not only Scottish Presbyterians from the old Kirk on Finch Road, but those of English antecedents from the demolished Finch Hill Church on Buck's Road, Douglas.

Top left: Willaston Methodist Church of 1960 on another Douglas Corporation estate.

Above left: The First Church of Christ Scientist, Douglas, a church and reading room for Christian Scientists in Woodbourne Road, Douglas.

Above: The Church of Jesus Christ of Latter-day Saints, Douglas, the place of worship in a leafy plot in upper Douglas of the denomination popularly known as Mormons.

This page and preceding pages: St Ninian's Church, built in 1913 at the highest point of Douglas (then right on the edge of the town, and also on the course of the TT motorbike races). It was designed by the important Arts and Crafts architect W D Caröe and was magnificently simple. The view on the preceding pages was taken before the regrettable closing off of the west end for meeting rooms, etc. It has always belonged to a notable Low Church tradition within the Church of England, the exact opposite of St Matthew's across the town. It was paid for by the trustees of the Island's great Victorian philanthropist, Henry Bloom Noble, and adjoins the public park which bears his name.

St Thomas' Church, Douglas, opened in 1849 as a fourth Anglican church for the growing town. Its internal appearance was transformed in the years before the Great War by the magnificent murals covering every wall surface. They are the work of the local artist John Miller Nicholson and depict a variety of Christian symbolism.

Above right: the Chancel floor dates from 1928; the spear and mason's square are a symbol of St Thomas.

61

St Thomas' Church, Douglas.

Right: The exterior from the sea; the main shopping street of the town leads off to the left. The Church is an early work of the prolific church architect Ewan Christian; it was intended to have a spire but the foundations turned out to be unsuitable.

Top left: More of J M Nicholson's murals; the symbols in the nave include a phoenix (on the left) and a dove.

Above: Nicholson's St Michael slaying the dragon, an inscription in mediaeval-style lettering below. The window dates from 1927.

Top left and top right: Loch Promenade Methodist Church, built on the Victorian seafront amid the boarding houses in 1976. It replaced a Victorian predecessor on the same site and (a great loss) the demolished Victoria Street Chapel. The V-shaped roof, the left side higher than the right, marks the street corner well, although the detailing is not the finest. The interior is functional, with chairs not pews.

Above and middle left: Salisbury Street Chapel, Douglas. One of the smaller urban chapels, it was built in 1891 and closed in 2009.

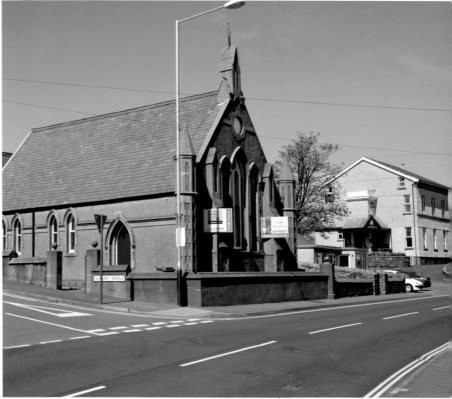

Top right: St Anthony's Roman Catholic Church, Onchan, which replaced a temporary structure in the 1980's.

Top left: The east window at St Anthony's, the figure of Christ etched on the glass by local artist Chris Spittall and seeming to walk on the water of Douglas Bay.

Above right: Onchan Methodist Chapel, designed for the Wesleyans by James Cowle, a prominent local architect, and opened in 1870; Gothic features are to the fore. It was replaced in the 1980's and is at the time of writing for to let/sale, painted primrose yellow.

Above left: The new Onchan Methodist Chapel, opened in 1987.

Onchan Church. One of the churches rebuilt during Bishop Ward's time, to the designs of the Welch brothers.

Left: These heads appear at Onchan both inside and out, and also on a country house where the Welches are believed to have worked, from where one was copied for Malew Church. The stonework shows horrendous ribbon pointing, misguided work of the twentieth century.

Top right: From the south, the original rural setting is easier to visualise. The church is not a simple rectangle as the older Manx churches were; the sanctuary projects out on the right.

Top left: In recent years the Manx Museum has remounted and relit the collection of Norse crosses.

Above left and middle left: A series of windows installed in 1971 and designed by the Manx architect Wilfred Quayle include depictions of other churches such as Ballaugh Old Church (with the text of the inscription on its font) and the Cathedral.

Above right: The interior is a mixture of work from all periods since the church was built, but generally working well together. The sanctuary, entered through three arches with columns in between, is the most elaborate in any Ward church. The pulpit is an early work by the Arts and Crafts architect M H Baillie Scott, who also designed the church hall; the wooden rood screen came later, in 1933, and was carved by Kelly Bros of Michael.

Lonan Old Church.

Left: The parish church until 1733, it was heavily restored in the 1890's by its vicar, the antiquarian and novelist Canon John Quine.

Top left and above left: The interior appears entirely Victorian; the stained glass included one window with some rather dubious heraldry.

Top right: This Norse cross in the churchyard is the only one on the Island possibly still in its original position.

Right: At some stage before the mid-nineteenth century the western half of the church lost its roof; it also escaped the worst of Victorian restoration, and the mediaeval fabric is thus more visible.

Top left and above left: St Luke's, Baldwin, built by Bishop Ward as a chapel-of-ease in the remote north of Braddan. It is similar to Dalby, although it has lost its original interior. In both, the west end was originally a schoolroom.

Right and top right: Christ Church, Laxey, of 1856, a chapel-of-ease to Lonan in this former mining village. It is in the style produced in quantity by Ewan Christian, based on a Yorkshire church from early in his career. On the Island, it is very like the larger Marown New Church. The patterned stained glass is attractive and works well in the narrow lancet windows.

Above: The interior of Lonan New Church, the simplest of the parish churches rebuilt under Bishop Ward in the 1830's, but still having a separate projecting sanctuary and two aisles The floor has been well-paved.

Left: Agneash Primitive Methodist Chapel, built in 1857 in a remote hamlet high in the Laxey valley. It retains its original interior, complete with box pews, and is an important survivor of so many which have been gutted for residential conversion.

Top left: Glen Road Wesleyan Methodist Chapel, Laxey, built in 1850. One of the grandest exercises in classical ecclesiastical architecture on the Island, if a rather unorthodox one. The tall windows with Gothick tracery are especially noteworthy. Now converted and in private hands.

Middle left: Baldrine Primitive Methodist Chapel of 1885. Typical of many rebuildings with Gothic windows; the previous chapel survives opposite.

Right and above: Christ Church the Dhoon. A chapel-of-ease to Maughold, but now in shared Anglican and Methodist use. Built in 1855 and possibly designed by Ewan Christian; it is a reworking of his familiar style in Romanesque not Gothic, and so with window and door openings round-headed not pointed. The interior is more predictable but charmingly untouched.

Maughold, one of the most ancient religious sites on the Island and possibly a monastery before the Viking conquest.

Previous pages: The exterior shows traces of early work in the Romanesque toothed arch over the door and the narrow Gothic windows half-way along the south wall, but otherwise it is coated in Victorian pebbledash.

Left: The Maughold Cross originally stood outside the churchyard gate and looks out of place in the church. It has been dated to the fourteenth century. It is carved with many symbols, including the chalice in the shield seen here; the significance of the whole scheme remains unclear, but is probably religious.

Top left: Memorial to the early twentieth century popular novelist Sir T H Hall Caine, by the Manx Art Nouveau designer Archibald Knox.

Top right: The interior now looks wholly Victorian as a result of a catastrophic 'restoration' of 1900.

Above left and right: In the late nineteenth century many largely-forgotten ancient stone crosses, mostly from the period of Viking rule, were collected together at the church of the parish where they were found. Maughold has an especially fine collection, housed in a cross-house designed by the local Arts and Crafts architect Armitage Rigby. In front, a small cross commemorating the Millennium in 2000 stands on a good 1930's Modern base designed for the Maughold Cross which stood there for a time.

Top left: The Ramsey showrooms of the Manx Electricity Authority were built in the 1880's by a small denomination called the Hallelujah Band (apparently not dissimilar to the Salvation Army). In 1890 it passed to the Methodist New Connexion, a group which had split from the mainstream at the end of the eighteenth century and merged with others to become the United Methodist Church in 1907; the chapel closed in the 1930's.

Middle left: Quayle's Hall, Ramsey, a fine building opened in 1837 to serve Scottish Presbyterians in the town; the iron windows are similar to those in the Anglican Ward churches of the time.

Top right: Waterloo Road Methodist Church, Ramsey, built in 1845 and probably designed by its builder, James Callow. By this date, much Victorian classicism, rather than looking directly to ancient Greece or Rome, was influenced by Italian buildings of the Renaissance.

Above: The Independent Methodist Chapel in Chapel Lane, Ramsey, one of the few survivors of the destruction of much of the old town in the late 1960's.Built in 1835 for the Primitive Methodists but transferred with part of its congregation to a smaller denomination, the Independent Methodists, in 1892. It has an atmospheric interior.

Right: Trinity United Reformed Church, Ramsey, an essay in Nonconformist Gothic from 1883-5, replacing what is now Quayle's Hall as the place of worship for Ramsey Presbyterians.

Left: Trinity United Reformed Church, Ramsey; the trio of organ, altar and pulpit dominate the interior, which is at first-floor level.

Top left: The former Glen Auldyn Primitive Methodist Chapel, now a private house.

Middle left: The Bethel in Ramsey, a mission to seafarers. The present building dates from 1973 and is reminiscent of the many bungalows built on the Island at that time; the roots of the mission in the town date back to the middle of the nineteenth century.

Top right: Ballure Chapel was the original (Anglican) chapel-of-ease for old Ramsey, a little way from the centre but advantageously so given the propensity for parts of the town to get washed away by the sea. It was repaired and altered over the years until (largely redundant after the opening of St Paul's in 1822) it was given a Victorian 'restoration' so thorough as to destroy anything of any historic interest. It was sold off in 200[ ] and is now a private house, although an area of the churchyard has had the gravestones moved into it and remains open to the public.

Above left: The former North Shore Road Wesleyan Chapel of 1891, which had a long association with the nearby children's home. It is an attractive building of some pretensions, which, especially with the porch bereft of the tower which should crown it, is comparable to the slightly later and larger Mount Tabor in Port St Mary.

Above right: St Fingan's Chapel, Glen Auldyn, originally a Wesleyan Chapel, but bought and converted to Anglican use in 1960 at the expense of the Yates family (of Wine Lodge fame) who had lived at Milntown at the base of the glen.

This page and preceding: St Paul's Church, Ramsey. Built from 1814-1822 to the designs of Thomas Brine, an architect who lived on the Island for the thirty years until his death in 1840, but unfortunately greatly altered since. The exterior, apart from the differences in the towers, originally looked more like Jurby Church does today. The interior would have been a plain rectangle with a ceiling and box pews. In 1844, north and south transepts and extra galleries were added, quite sympathetically, to provide more seating. Over the next seventy years, other changes were made to make the interior look more Gothic and less classical, influenced by the clergy who were Anglo-Catholic. The current interior mixes classical proportions and gallery-fronts with Victorian tiles, stained glass and furnishings. Some of the woodwork has been painted white while the rest remains dark brown. The modern, light-wood nave altar (above) adds another layer.

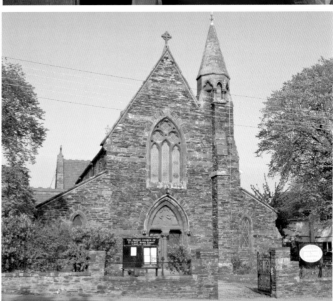

This page and preceding: St Olave's, North Ramsey, one of the most successful Victorian churches on the Island. It was built in the 1860's and designed by a London architect, Michael Manning. Many enhancements have been made to the interior over the years, but they are sympathetic to the original design and so meld into an harmonious whole.

The wrought iron screen (preceding page) is a war memorial from the Great War; the matching corona (top right), the chancel light fitting, was made in Peel in 1979.

Middle left: These windows are by John Hayward, one of the best stained glass designers of the later twentieth century; there are others at Bride. On the right is St Nicholas, on the left St Maughold carrying the coracle in which he was supposed to have been cast adrift, only to be washed up on the headland bearing his name.

Above left: The walls are built of local stone with all the carved work ('dressed' stone) in red sandstone from Whitehaven.

Right: Our Lady Star of the Sea and St Maughold (see overleaf).

(This page and preceding): The Roman Catholic church of Our Lady Star of the Sea and St Maughold, a mouthful of a name but one of the finest churches on the Island. It is an early work of Giles Gilbert Scott and was built in 1909-10. It is tall and spacious internally, as a Roman Catholic church of the day had to be, but the baptistry (middle left) is low and intimate; the stars around the altar are, like those throughout the interior, a tribute to the 'Star of the Sea'. The church is built of local stone, but with a roof of rust-coloured tiles, unlike the slates which were customary on the Island. The interior is lined with bricks from St John's.

The reredos over the high altar (preceding page) was, like most of the fittings, also designed by Scott; it is in the form of a triptych in which the side panels are hinged and so can be brought forward to close it up when liturgical practice demands. The paintings are by Frances Burlison.

Right: Lezayre Church was rebuilt in 1835 as one of Bishop Ward's new churches, and designed by the Welch brothers. It is in a most attractive setting between the hills and the northern plain.

Top left: The interior of Lezayre Church, from the gallery. Like the other Ward churches, it is mostly one large undivided space, with a small projecting sanctuary containing the altar. Where the organ is on the left and the small Lady Chapel on the right were originally the large box pews of the two principal families of the parish. There are two aisles to allow easier access, a feature the ecclesiologists would soon anathematise as insufficiently reverent to the altar.

Middle left: Leodest Primitive Methodist Chapel, dating from 1835, out in the fields north of Andreas village. To lovers of simplicity, one of the most beautiful of the chapels with its plain whitewashed walls and low hipped roof. It is notable for retaining (at the time of writing) its original interior, although it has been disused for some years.

Above left: Andreas church at dawn. The tower was once much taller but was reduced in height when Andreas airfield was built in the Second World War.

Andreas Church. Now largely Victorian in appearance as a result of substantial additions, there is in fact the shell of a late Georgian building underneath.

Left: the church is approached up two long drives, and where they join is a green with the tall and powerful War Memorial.

Top left: Sandulf's Cross, from the tenth century, used to stand in the churchyard but is now inside; note the interlacing pattern at the bottom.

Above left: The remarkable rose window high on the east wall contains in the centre a knight embarked on the ship of Faith, surrounded by the signs of the zodiac.

Above right: The interior, perhaps the most successful adaptation on the Island of an older church to Victorian requirements. The raised roof gives a sense of space, and the windows admit plenty of light. The pale-coloured graining of the pews is unusual but successful.

Top: Bride Church was completely rebuilt in 1869-76 to the designs of Joseph Henry Christian, who worked in the office of his better-known cousin Ewan and seems to have produced the more original of the firm's work on the Island. At any rate Bride is an example of a modest but successful Victorian village church. The two windows visible at the west end are by John Hayward, the distinguished designer who died in 2007 and is perhaps best known for the great west window at Sherborne Abbey.

Below: The present church at Jurby is a Regency building, by the Manx architect John Taggart. With white walls and red sandstone dressings, it was copied by St Paul's, Ramsey, but in turn may have been based on the old church (now largely demolished) at Michael. It is perched on Jurby Head and is a well-known landmark, visible from afar.

It was altered in 1939-40 by another Manx architect, Wilfred Quayle, who shortened the tower and gave it is present rather Mediterranean-looking pyramidal cap. He added a brown brick porch in a modern style (just visible on the left of the exterior view) and reordered the interior. The result is one of the most interesting twentieth-century creations on the Island.

Top left: St Jude's, an Anglican chapel-of-ease in the curragh country of southern Andreas, is one of Bishop Ward's churches of the 1830's and ranks in size midway between the large parish churches and the small chapels such as Dalby. It has recently been immaculately restored by the Friends of St Jude's, a charity set up by local people when the Church of England tried to demolish it. It retains its original pews and ceiling.

Above left: Ballaugh Old Church is one of the Island's ancient parish churches, of mediaeval origin. It was extended westwards in 1717 when the charming cupola was added, but in 1849, after a new church had been built, the older, eastern part was demolished. It is notable for its reddish hue, much of which is in fact due to coloured mortar.

Top right: Ballaugh New Church is one of those built from funds raised by Bishop Ward in the 1830's. The architects were the Welch brothers; the tower, with an octagonal `lantern' on a square base, was a common design of the time, based originally on Boston Stump in Lincolnshire; nearer Ballaugh, St Mary's in Castletown had the same arrangement. Like many early Gothic revival churches, the windows are narrow, pointed lancets.

Right: The interior of Ballaugh New Church is typical of its period, consisting of a single, wide space without arches partitioning any of it off. A gallery provides extra seating, and, on the standard Ward church pattern, there are two aisles giving easy access to all pews (these are Victorian replacements) .

Jurby airfield 3m
Jurby Nurseries and 4½m
Water Gardens

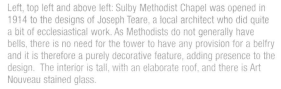

Left, top left and above left: Sulby Methodist Chapel was opened in 1914 to the designs of Joseph Teare, a local architect who did quite a bit of ecclesiastical work. As Methodists do not generally have bells, there is no need for the tower to have any provision for a belfry and it is therefore a purely decorative feature, adding presence to the design. The interior is tall, with an elaborate roof, and there is Art Nouveau stained glass.

Top right and right: Bishopscourt was the palace of the Bishops of Sodor and Man from the thirteenth century until 1974 when a new bishop refused to live there and decamped to Ramsey. The mediaeval chapel was demolished in 1825, but only three decades later its replacement was converted to an ante-room for a much larger new chapel, dedicated to St Nicholas and designed by W G Habershon, a minor Victorian church architect (who had very tenuous Manx connections as his father had trained the prolific Ewan Christian). It was designated pro-cathedral of the diocese as St German's in Peel Castle was in ruins. Bishopscourt is now a private house.

Michael Church. Another of the churches rebuilt under Bishop Ward in the 1830's to the designs of the Welch brothers. It is an effective and varied composition, built of local slate and rendered the colour of Bath stone; the tower dominates the village. Inside, the plan, which is T-shaped with a small sanctuary opposite the upright of the T, has adapted very well to modern forms of worship. The whole church has recently been redecorated very successfully, in sympathy with the original design.

Above: The reredos behind the altar was painted by the wife of a former vicar.

Top left: The church now contains an important collection of Norse crosses mainly from the eleventh century, for many years in the lych-gate. On the left is the Dragon Cross with accomplished interlacing.

Top left: The first Primitive Methodist chapel in Michael, built in 1824 and used until 1868; now commercial premises.

Top right: Michael Methodist Chapel, built by the Primitive Methodists in 1868 and a very handsome example of simple Victorian classical design. The large central window is a variation of a Venetian window, a mainstay of classical design, but normally with the sidelights flat-headed, not rounded. Much of the original interior survives.

Middle left: Spooyt Vane Mission Hall. In a rural area in the south of the parish and possibly dating from the second quarter of the nineteenth century, with attractive iron windows. An Anglican establishment.

Above: The lychgate leading into Michael churchyard, designed by the Arts and Crafts architect Armitage Rigby as a home for the parish's Viking crosses, now moved inside the church for greater protection.

Top: Barregarrow Methodist Chapel, on the TT course where the road up the hills to Brandywell leaves the main road from Castletown to Ramsey. Built in 1880 and originally Wesleyan; the original interior survives.

Above: the former Anglican chapel-of-ease at Cronk-y-Voddey in the uplands of German parish, built in 1852 to serve an area remote from the parish church at Peel. Now converted to a private house.

St German's, Peel, built in 1879-84 by Bishop Hill who had a hankering for a cathedral with a roof. It was simply a (very grand) chapel-of-ease to St Peter's until it became the parish church of German in 1893. In 1980 it was declared the new cathedral, but, while it is used for diocesan events, national ceremonies tend now to be held at St John's. It is a heavy design, and its internal appearance has not been assisted by an unsuccessful reordering; another is overdue.

Top left: The arms of the diocese of Sodor and Man; the figure is St Mary the Virgin.

Top right: There was originally a spire but it had to be taken down in 1907 when the tower started to subside.

Middle left: Moses, Isaiah and Jeremiah in the chancel, painted by the Manx nineteenth-century artist John Millar Nicholson (who also painted the murals at St Thomas', Douglas).

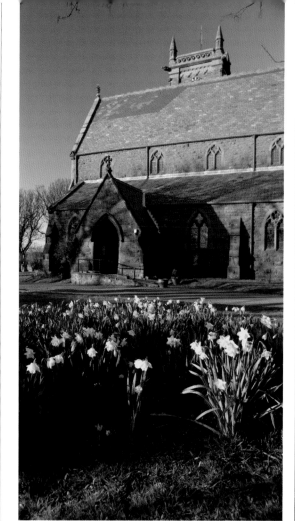

St German's, Peel.

The glass display cases (above right) were added at the west end after the building became a cathedral, to house church plate from various parts of the Island; the bright internal lighting might have made a less prominent location more advisable.

The war memorial (above) stands on a green between St German's and the narrow entrance to Atholl Street; it was carved by T H Royston, the Douglas monumental mason responsible for many gravestones of the period.

Top left: Only the façade of the former Primitive Methodist Chapel of 1878 in Christian Street, Peel, survives, now attached to a block of flats.

Middle left: The Elim Pentecostal Church, Peel, a fine classical building erected in the 1840's as the Mathematical School, which closed in 1892. It was for a time a Baptist church and was extensively restored in 1997, but is now Pentecostal.

Top right: The Centenary Centre, a Peel arts venue, originally the Centenary Hall, so called because the chapel it served was built in 1839, the hundredth anniversary of the Methodist Union.

Above: Peel Centenary Methodist Church, Atholl Street. Originally Wesleyan, it has a handsome classical facade and this splendid galleried interior. The gallery survives with its original pews but the ground floor has unfortunately been altered.

Top left: St Patrick's Church on St Patrick's Isle, dating from the eleventh century and officially the parish church of Patrick until 1714 (the boundary between Patrick and German ran across the islet).

Top right: The Cathedral, in an outstanding position on St Patrick's Isle, was also theoretically the parish church of German until 1880. Within the walls of Peel Castle, it suffered depredations as a convenient source of building material for military purposes, and the last of its roof blew off in the early nineteenth century. It is a Gothic structure, the earliest part dating from the thirteenth century. Money raised for its restoration was used to build the Victorian St German's Church on the mainland, which was declared the cathedral in its place in 1980.

Above left: St Peter's Church, Peel, a building of some antiquity, as the rounded shape of its churchyard (visible in this view) suggests. It was officially a chapel-of-ease to the cathedral until 1880, but acted as the parish church of German and (until 1714) Patrick, too. It was much altered and extended over the years, the tower being added in 1872. The church was largely demolished in 1958, except for the tower; only low walls remain, in which a mediaeval piscina is still visible.

Right: In St Peter's churchyard, but not in its proper place; after the destruction of much of the church, all the gravestones were taken up and rearranged.

Top left and right: St Patrick's Roman Catholic Church, Peel, built in 1865, slightly outside the town centre to avoid anti-catholic feeling.

Middle left and above: St John's Methodist Chapel, originally Wesleyan and dating from 1824, although much altered. All the other chapels in the area closed by the end of the 1970's, leaving St John's to serve a large part of the centre of the Island.

St John's Church. Since 1948 an Anglican parish church serving much of the rural part of the parish of German, but built to replace a predecessor which had been more courthouse than chapel. It was designed by the Manchester architect Richard Lane and built in 1849.

Top left: The west door of the church leads onto a processional way to the Tynwald Hill.

Middle and above left: It is the venue for a service at the beginning of the time-honoured open-air sitting of the Tynwald Court, the Manx national assembly, and special seats at the crossing are marked for the various members.

Right: The chancel has a good floor of Minton encaustic tiles.

Top right: the former Foxdale Village Wesleyan Methodist Chapel, on the main road in the former mining village. Probably mid-Victorian and now a private house.

Above: Foxdale Church (St Paul's), opened in 1876 as a chapel-of-ease to Patrick, being given its own parish in 1881; Foxdale had previously been divided between Patrick, Marown and Malew. It was designed by James Cowle, a local architect responsible for many of the `baronial meets boarding house' buildings of the time. It is an austere building, well-suited perhaps to its original setting in a harsh industrial environment.

Top left: Glen Maye Primitive Methodist Chapel of 1868, one of the most attractive exteriors on the Island, a classical building sitting quietly half way up the steep hill in this small western village.

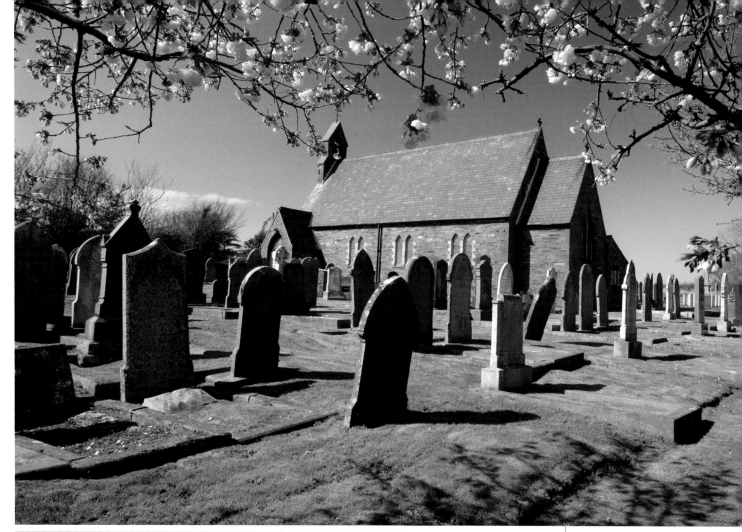

Patrick Church. Built in 1879-81 just for funerals as it was intended to build a new parish church more centrally at Glen Maye. Its erection necessitated the destruction of its predecessor dating from 1714. It is a modest structure of no architectural pretensions.

Above left: There was a large internment camp just across the road at Knockaloe in the Great War, and there are therefore many war graves in the churchyard.

Right: The Victorian interior is largely unchanged, with pitch-pine pews and exposed roof timbers.

BEHOLD A SOWER WENT FORTH TO SOW

TO THE GLORY OF GOD AND IN LOVING MEMORY OF
RICHARD QUIRK J P CP JUNE 10 1892 AGED 87

BEHOLD THE BRIDEGROOM COMETH

TO THE GLORY OF GOD AND IN LOVING MEMORY OF
RICHARD STEPHEN QUIRK MAY 7 1874 AGED 39
ELIZ' COLLARD JAN'Y 28 1873 AGED 39

Left: Window in Patrick Church, probably 1890's.

Top left: Zion Primitive Methodist Chapel at Bradda East near Port Erin.

Middle left: The former Ronague Wesleyan Chapel of 1869, now a private house (and recently extended in a rather ecclesiastical style)

Above left: Ballafesson Wesleyan Methodist Chapel near Port Erin, dating from 1798 and thus one of the oldest surviving chapels, although much altered externally over the years. The ventilator on the roof is charming (there were two the same on Malew Church up until 1929).

Top right: Ballabeg Methodist Chapel, Arbory - on the left the old chapel of 1854, now a hall, and on the right its successor of 1900.

Right: Inside Ballabeg Chapel, its 1900 interior well-preserved.

Arbory Church. Rebuilt in 1757-9 in a plain Georgian style.

Left: The tower was added in 1911 to the designs of Joseph Teare (the architect of Sulby Methodist Chapel)

Above left: The Sumner's Pulpit where that church functionary made announcements in days gone by.

Above right: Looking west. The gallery-front retains panelling probably from the 1760's.

Below: Looking east. On the walls can be seen some of the fine Georgian marble memorials. The pulpit on the left is by Wilfred Quayle, architect of the remodelling of Jurby. The garish east window is an unfortunate addition of the 1930's.

St Columba's Roman Catholic Church, Port Erin, a very plain modern building, subsequently extended to form an L-shape. The stained glass windows came from Finch Hill United Reformed Church, Douglas on its demolition.

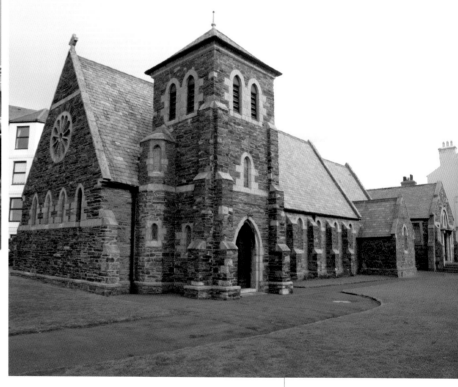

Top left: the Erin Arts Centre, Port Erin, formerly a Wesleyan Methodist Chapel, dating from 1911 and situated just off the seafront of this former watering place. The sculpture in the blocked-up doorway, commissioned by the Arts Centre, is of a Viking warrior with an array of shields, a fine work by Michael Sandle R.A.

Top right: Port Erin Methodist Church (formerly the Primitive Methodist chapel), built in 1901-3 to the designs of the Halifax architect W C Williams. The arrangement with the pulpit above the altar is typically Methodist.

Above left, right and overleaf: St Catherine's Church, Port Erin, a chapel-of-ease to Rushen Church built in 1880 to the designs of James Cowle who was working on Foxdale Church at the same time.

Rushen Church - or more correctly, Kirk Christ (the Manx way of saying Holy Trinity) in Rushen Sheading.

Previous page: The war memorial lychgate now shelters one of the earliest gravestones on the Island

Left: Like so many of the Manx Georgian churches, it has an attractive cupola'd bell-turret. The plastic windows are unfortunate.

Top left: Lecterns were a Victorian innovation; previously the parson read the lessons from his desk.

Top right: The three-sided ('canted') apse was added in 1869 to make more room for (or give greater prominence to) the altar

Above left: This window commemorates William Milner, the Victorian safe-maker and benefactor of the local poor. Putting stained glass in a Georgian window like this allowed more of a picture to be composed than in Gothic windows.

Right: In the churchyard; most here are of the local limestone.

Next pages: Looking west. The Georgian gallery-front has lost its supporting columns.

St Peter's Cregneash, a chapel-of-ease to Rushen built in 1878 to serve the people of this upland crofting village, much of it now a folk museum. It is a good approximation externally of an old Manx chapel, with a restrained Victorian interior.

Right: A window showing a reconstruction of the Calf of Man Crucifixion, a stone panel, probably an altar-front, found on the Calf, the small island off the coast just south-west of Cregneash. It dates from the period of Viking rule on the Island, sometime before or after the year 1000.

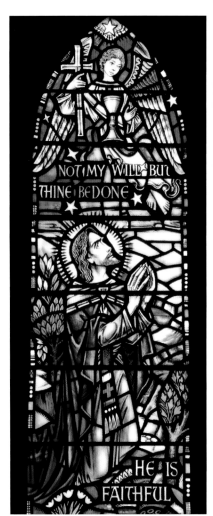

St Mary's, Port St Mary, another chapel-of-ease to Rushen, built in 1884 to serve the people of the fishing port. It is largely unaltered internally and externally except for the striking modern windows.

HY WILL BE DONE ON EARTH

Top: Another view of the modern windows at St Mary's, Port St Mary.

Above left: The new Baptist Church in Port St Mary, built to replace a former Methodist chapel which had developed structural problems. Electronic equipment is displayed openly on a stage and not hidden away behind woodwork. The large window is especially striking with the morning sun shining in.

Right: Malew Church from the north-east showing the Chancel, rebuilt in 1781, and the 'Wing' or north transept added on two years later, giving the church the T-plan ideal for an auditory church, where everyone needed to hear the parson.

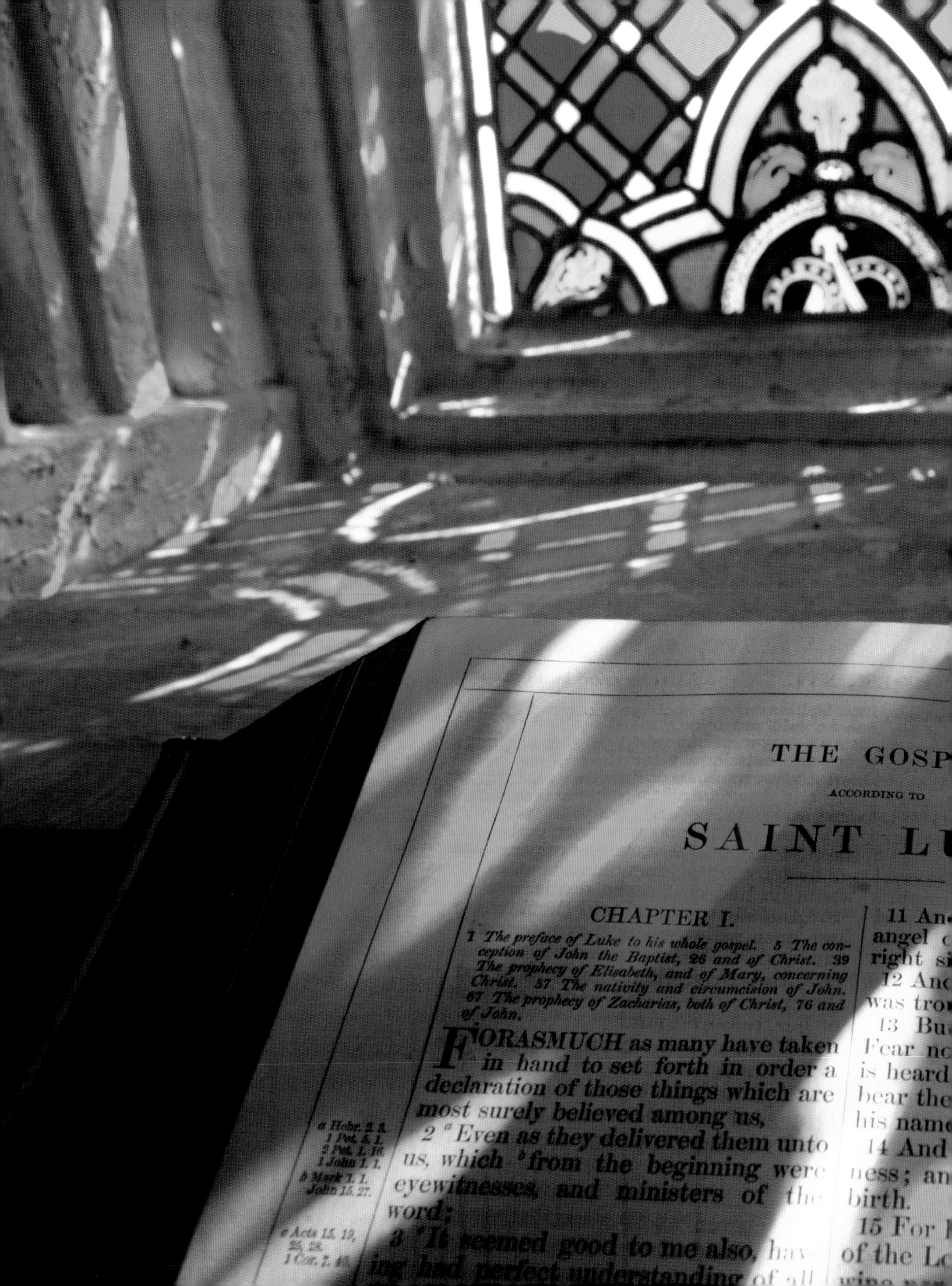

THE GOSP

ACCORDING TO

SAINT LU

CHAPTER I.

1 The preface of Luke to his whole gospel. 5 The conception of John the Baptist, 26 and of Christ. 39 The prophecy of Elisabeth, and of Mary, concerning Christ. 57 The nativity and circumcision of John. 67 The prophecy of Zacharias, both of Christ, 76 and of John.

^a Hebr. 2. 3.
1 Pet. 5. 1.
2 Pet. 1. 16.
1 John 1. 1.
^b Mark 1. 1.
John 15. 27.

^c Acts 15. 19,
20, 22.
1 Cor. 7. 10.

FORASMUCH as many have taken in hand to set forth in order a declaration of those things which are most surely believed among us,

2 ^aEven as they delivered them unto us, which ^bfrom the beginning were eyewitnesses, and ministers of the word;

3 ^cIt seemed good to me also, having had perfect understanding of all

11 And
angel o
right si
12 And
was trou
13 Bu
Fear no
is heard
bear the
his name
14 And
ness; an
birth.
15 For
of the L

E.

appeared unto him an
Lord standing on the
the altar of incense.
Zacharias saw *him*, [h]e
nd fear fell upon him.
angel said unto him,
arias: for thy prayer
y wife Elisabeth shall
, and [p] thou shalt call

alt have joy and glad.
y shall rejoice at his

be great in the sight
shall drink

Before the
Account
called An-
no Domini
the sixth
Year.

b See 2 Kings
11. 5.
1 Chron. 9,
25.

c Gen. 30, 23.
Isai. 4. 1.
& 54. 1, 4.

d Matt. 1. 18.
ch. 2, 4, 5.

e Dan. 9, 23.
& 10, 19.

ceived that he had seen a vision in
the temple: for he beckoned unto
them, and remained speechless.

23 And it came to pass, that, as soon
as [b] the days of his ministration were
accomplished, he departed to his own
house.

24 And after those days his wife
Elisabeth conceived, and hid herself
five months, saying,

25 Thus hath the Lord dealt with
me in the days wherein he looked on
me, to [c] take away my reproach among
men.

26 And in the sixth month the angel
Gabriel was sent from God unto a city
of Galilee, named Nazareth,

27 To a virgin [d] espoused to a man
whose name was Joseph, of the house
of David; and the virgin's name *was*
Mary.

28 And the angel came in unto her,
and said, [e] Hail, *thou that art* [f] highly
favoured, *f* the Lord is

57 For [q] with God nothing shall be
impossible.

38 And Mary said, Behold the hand
maid of the Lord; be it unto me a
cording to thy word. And the an
departed from her.

39 And Mary arose in those
and went into the hill country
haste, [r] into a city of Juda:

40 And entered into the ho
Zacharias, and saluted Elisa

41 And it came to pass, th
Elisabeth heard the sal
Mary, the babe leaped in
and Elisabeth was fill
Holy Ghost:

42 And she spake o
voice, and said, [s]
among women, an
fruit of thy womb.

43 And whence *is*
mother of my Lo

44 For l

Malew Church.

Previous pages: Light shining through the east window of 1842, the first on the Island in modern times. The WW mark of the maker, William Wailes of Newcastle, can be seen on the right.

Top left: The bells in the bell-cote which rises above the mediaeval west end.

Middle left: The sundial of 1835; almost all the old parish churches have one.

Top right: A fragment of woodwork from about 1500, conceivably part of a rood screen. On the right are the three legs of Mann, on the left an eagle's foot, badge of Lord Monteagle, one of the Stanley family which then ruled the Island.

Above: The war memorial window of 1922 by the Irish academician Kathleen Shaw.

VICARS OF MALEW
SINCE 1919
SYDNEY BENSON BOTWOOD 1919
ROBERT HIGGINSON REID 1931
HENRY SAUNDERSON 1932
HENRY SMITH WHITTAKER 1934
WILLIAM HENRY SAUNDERS 1949

Malew Church.

Above: In the 'Wing', the addition of 1783, which forms the upright of the T-shaped plan. The pews are original and are raked for better visibility.

Right: Looking west from the chancel towards the galleries. Note the rounded corner of the box pew on the right.

Left: The mediaeval west end of Malew Church, much altered over succeeding centuries, notably by the insertion of large Georgian windows. The grave-monuments against the wall are fine early-nineteenth century work.

This page: St Mary's on the Harbour, Castletown, built in 1838 as a school, later church rooms and finally a church on the ground floor and a hall above.

Top left: A window showing the first chapel in the town, now the Old Grammar School.

Top right: It is built, like Castle Rushen opposite, of the local Castletown limestone.

Above left: The altar was a Victorian addition to the previous church, St Mary's, gutted in the 1980's.

Right: The church as originally laid out, with the altar on the left so as to face east. A more logical lay-out has now been adopted.

Top left: The Band Room in Queen Street, Castletown, now the home of the Metropolitan Silver Band but opened in 1896 as the Queen Street Mission ('Protestant and Evangelical'), an œcumenical initiative by Church and Chapel.

Middle left: The Old Grammar School, Castletown, was the first of four St Mary's to serve the old capital. It was a chapel-of-ease to Malew Church and dates from the thirteenth century. The extension on the right is late seventeenth century, the building having been used as a school from 1698 to 1931. It is now in the ownership of the Manx Museum and functions as a tourist information centre.

Top right: The former Primitive Methodist Chapel in Malew Street, Castletown, dating from 1893. It is of typical 'Prim' pattern, with the chapel itself at first floor level.

Above: Above: Castletown Methodist Church in Arbory Street, originally Wesleyan, with the chapel at ground level. It was built in 1833, but the interior was greatly altered in 1890 when the chancel was added, originally containing choirstalls.

St Mary's Roman Catholic Church, built on the outskirts of Castletown in 1828, a more central location being then politically unacceptable.

Above: It contains the finest stained glass on the Island, two windows by the great Dublin artist Harry Clarke (1889-1931).

Top right: The interior was altered in both the 1920's and 1980's.

Right: Some of the original Georgian interior survives, notably the Gothick windows, the gallery columns and the ceiling.

St Thomas' Chapel, King William's College, a public school just outside Castletown, founded in 1833.The new chapel was built in 1878-9 to the designs of the Manx architect James Cowle.

Left: The elaborate canopied stalls and inward-facing benches give the impression of a cathedral quire or the chapel of a college at one of the Universities.

Top left: The first chapel was in a wing of the main building; the upper part is now the Barrovian Hall.

Above left: The Chapel on the right; the main block of the school looks itself like a great church.

Top right: The east window, in memory of Bishop Barrow who founded the College's predecessor the Academic School (in fact more of an tertiary institution).

Right: The frescoes in the chancel with scenes of the life of St Thomas.

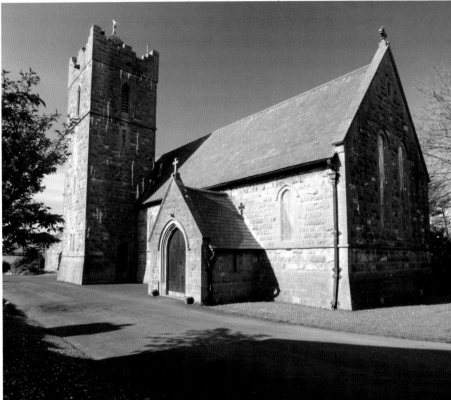

Left: St Michael's Chapel on Fort Island, Derbyhaven. Dating from the twelfth century, it is a little larger than the field churches the scanty remains of which are dotted about the Manx countryside, but it gives an idea of what they would have looked like.

Top left: The ruins of Rushen Abbey, a Cistercian monastery at Ballasalla founded in 1134. The tower is a later mediaeval insertion into the then-existing church ; the arcading in the foreground is a modern reproduction 'interpreting' the site.

Above left, top right and right: St Mary's Church, Ballasalla, a chapel-of-ease to Malew Church and known as the Abbey Church to distinguish it from the myriad other churches in the area with the same dedication, but having no connection with Rushen Abbey other than its situation a few hundred yards away. It was a very late work of Ewan Christian (or his office) and built in 1895-7. The interior is largely-untouched Edwardian, all of a piece.

Top left: Ballasalla Village Hall, formerly known as the Church House, built at the expense of William Cain, a rich Melbourne builder of local origins.

Middle left: The old village school in Ballasalla, dating from 1843, used as a meeting place by local Methodists in the early twenty-first century following the demolition of their chapel which had become unsafe. They now use the Abbey Church.

Top right, above and right: St Mark's Chapel, another chapel-of-ease to Malew, built in 1772 in the north of the large parish, where a hamlet has since taken its name. It has the elaborate bell-turret of so many Manx Georgian churches. The font (top right) is of local granite.

Overleaf: The interior of St Mark's. None of the fittings is original, but they achieve a pleasant effect.

Preceding pages: Santan Church, very like St Mark's, with which it is contemporary; it was rebuilt or remodelled in 1774. It is typical of Manx eighteenth century church architecture with its bell-turret, round-headed windows and little pinnacles on the corners.

Santan Church.

Preceding pages: The exterior is very like St Mark's, with which it is contemporary; it was rebuilt or remodelled in 1774. It is typical of Manx eighteenth century church architecture with its bell-turret, round-headed windows and little pinnacles on the corners.

Top left: Looking west. The woodwork is unusually dark, but each church chose its own shade. On the front of the gallery are the Royal Arms, once found in every church.

Top right: The insensitive insertion of modern light wood at the east end spoils what is otherwise a superbly-preserved Georgian interior; it would not be difficult to restore the interior to its full glory. The blue colour-scheme is attractive.

Above: A detail from the east window, depicting the last supper; it is by the well-known Lancaster firm of Shrigley and Hunt and is extremely conservative for its date, 1952.

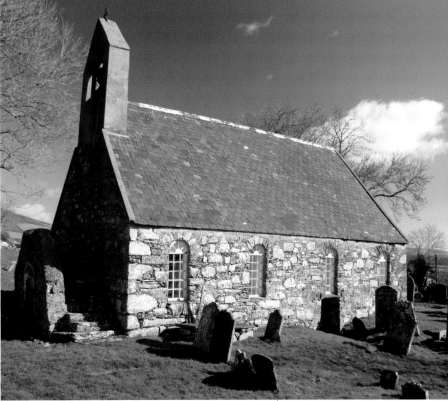

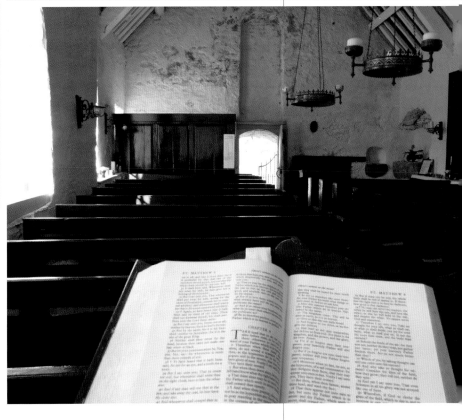

This page and next pages: Marown Old Church, perhaps the most quietly atmospheric of all the Island's churches. It is of ancient origins, but much of the oldest (eastern) part was demolished in the 1850's after the new church had been built.

Top left: The white-painted roof timbers give the interior a very light feel.

Top right: The present west end was added in the 1750's, with outside steps to a now-vanished gallery.

Above left: There are two fonts, possibly mediaeval, although the smaller may have been a holy water stoup, containing water with which to make the sign of the cross before the Reformation. There are a number of these granite 'fonts' throughout the Island; at least some may have started life as mortars or in some other secular use.

Right: The blocked-up door to the former gallery can be seen above the entrance door.

Overleaf: Looking west; there is no jarring note to the unspoiled patina of age.

Top left: Crosby Methodist Chapel, built in 1833 by the Revd Robert Aitken, a highly-eccentric figure who was ordained an Anglican clergyman but flirted with Methodism. He built Eyreton Castle nearby, and the chapel is battlemented, too.

Above right: An Art Nouveau window in Crosby Chapel.

Middle left: Marown New Church was started in 1849 and consecrated in 1853 to replace the old parish church up the hill. It may have been designed by Ewan Christian, the architect of St Thomas', Douglas, built at the same time; it is certainly in the standardised style Christian adopted, based on a Yorkshire church.

Above: The interior of Marown New Church, showing the pews with short half-doors so popular in the Isle of Man in the second half of the nineteenth century. Note the very steeply-pitched roof and the exposed timbers.

Above left: The former Union Mills Wesleyan Methodist Chapel of 1863, now a private house. It is one of the most striking ecclesiastical buildings on the Island, dominated by its great gable; while the ogee shape at the top is a Gothic moulding, the overall effect is more exotic, perhaps vaguely Turkish-looking; certainly not what one would associate with sober, respectable Victorian Methodists.

Top left, top right and right: The new Methodist Chapel in Union Mills, erected in 1930. It is low and undemonstrative in design (a reaction to its predecessor) and looks more like a hall than a chapel.

Left: The Dalrymple Memorial Chapel, Union Mills. The Congregationalists were never a significant denomination in the Isle of Man, and this is the only one of their buildings still in existence. It was built in 1863 to the designs of the good local architect John Robinson, responsible for much of the best of Victorian Douglas. The spire is reminiscent, on a much smaller scale, of Lezayre Church. It closed in 1930 and is now offices.

Above left: The first Wesleyan chapel at the Cooil in Braddan, built in 1834 and still domestic and Georgian in appearance.

Top right and right: The present Cooil Chapel, showing how as the nineteenth century progressed the Methodists adopted simplified Gothic features such as the pointed windows.

Previous pages: Old Kirk Braddan, the Island's only untouched Georgian church, although one with much older roots. In the churchyard, note the classically-inspired monument in the form of a pedestal crowned with a draped urn, a symbol of mourning.

Top: Top: The only part of Old Kirk Braddan where the original interior has been compromised is here, where a display has been made of the Celtic and Norse crosses found in the parish. Above: In the old churchyard at Braddan, with a variety of differently-shaped headstones.

Right: New Kirk Braddan which replaced the old church in 1876. It was designed by John Loughborough Pearson, one of the most prominent church architects of the day, whose wife was Manx. The spire blew down in 1884 and it is unfortunate that the top of the tower has still not been finished off in any way; battlements or a simple parapet would be a great improvement.

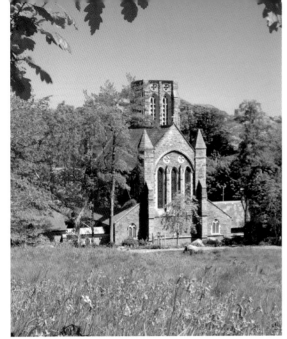

New Kirk Braddan.

Left: The interior, looking east to the altar in a semi-circular apse. It is the greatest Victorian interior on the Island, with great height and nobility. Note the contrast of the materials: brick to line the walls, Bath stone for the columns and timber for the roof. Speakers for modern sound systems can be intrusive if not well-placed.

Top left: The church from above, where open-air services for tourists were held in the season in the early twentieth century.

Middle left: Much of the stained glass is by the well-known firm of Clayton & Bell.

Top right: The War Memorial Chapel, designed by the Manx architect Wilfred Quayle.

Above left: Mosaic on the floor; some may be the work of the Arts and Crafts architect M H Baillie Scott, inspired by Pearson.

Right: The altar decked for a wedding.

MANX CHURCH AND CHAPEL ORGANS

CHAPTER THREE

Manx churches and chapels are graced by a wide variety of organs, from grand instruments in big town churches to the humblest harmoniums in small country chapels. Since they were introduced to the Island in the middle of the nineteenth century, they have played an important part in church and chapel life; the Manx are a Celtic race, and love to sing.

To add an extra dimension to this book, Manx-born organist Gareth Moore recorded on a selection of these organs over the winter of 2008/2009; the resulting CD can be found at the back of the book. The pieces Gareth chose are by composers as diverse as Bach, Widor and the Tashkent-based Georgi Mushel, and include some traditional Manx tunes.

The recordings were made by Charles Guard and the CD is sponsored by the Manx Heritage Foundation. The pieces and instruments featured are:

Track:

1. Introduction and Menuet by Louis Boëllman
    King William's College, Castletown
2. Prelude in Classic Style by Gordon Young
    St Mary's Catholic Church, Douglas
3. Prelude and Fugue in A Major by J S Bach – Crosby
    Methodist Chapel
4. Improvisation and The Good Old Way (Manx trad) –
    Abbeylands Methodist Chapel
5. Concerto in A Minor by Vivaldi arranged J S Bach – Kirk
    Michael Parish Church
6. War March of the Priests by Felix Mendelssohn – Peel
    Methodist Church
7. Variations on a 17th Century Manx Chorale (extract) by J
    E Quayle – Rushen Parish Church
8. Chorale Prelude: Wenn wir in höchsten Nöthen sein by J S
    Bach – Marown Parish Church
9. March on a Theme by Handel by Alexandre Guilmant –
    St Ninian's, Douglas
10. Toccata by Georgi Mushel – St George's Parish Church,
    Douglas
11. Choral Song by S S Wesley – St Paul's Church, Ramsey
12. Hymn: Hyfrydol and Prelude No. III by Ralph Vaughan
    Williams – St Thomas's, Douglas
13. Solemn Melody by Walford Davies (arr Rawsthorne) –
    Trinity Methodist Church, Douglas
14. Gavotte by S S Wesley – Sulby Methodist Church

Gareth Moore

15. Marche Pontificale by C M Widor – St Matthews,
    Douglas

All the recording sessions were attended by the Island's resident organ builder, Peter Jones, who was on hand to make any fine adjustments in tuning that were required to make sure that the instruments were at their best.

Peter, who has been working on the Island since 1979 and is currently responsible for the regular maintenance of all the Island's instruments, has researched the history of the Island's church and chapel organs and has supplied the following brief notes about them:

In 2009 there are around fifty-five instruments on the Island, including 5 house organs, and they include instruments from well-known English builders such as Forster and Andrews, Hill, Norman and Beard, Brindley and Foster and Harrison. We also have organs of lesser-known makers, such as Wadsworth, Hewitt, Keats, and those of builders almost confined to the Island, particularly Morgan and myself.

Moses Morgan was particularly interesting as his earliest

Top left: Crosby Methodist Chapel.

Top Right: King William's College, Castletown.

Middle Left: Abbeylands Chapel, Onchan.

Middle Right: : St Mary's Catholic Church, Douglas.

Above Left: Kirk Michael Parish Church.

Right: Peel Methodist Church.

instrument (Andreas Parish Church, 1898) was the first of a dozen or more organs he was responsible for over a fourteen-year period – a remarkable record of almost one instrument per year. Morgan arrived on the Island as an experienced builder, and presumably must have built other instruments in the UK. He was obviously a successful businessman, and ran a boarding house alongside the organ-building and piano tuning and supply enterprise. He was based at 12A St George's Walk.

The instruments featured on the CD are:

KING WILLIAM'S COLLEGE, CASTLETOWN

Great: 8,8,8,4,4,2,II,8; Swell: 8,8,8,8,4,2,16,8,4; Pedal: 16,16,16,8,4.

The College organ started life in 1906 when it was built for the Malew Street Methodist Church, Castletown, by Morgan and/or Pollard. In the 1970s the church closed and Laycock and Bannister of Yorkshire replaced the organ's mechanism with an electro-pneumatic one, and rebuilt it in its present form, with the Great to the left and the Swell to the right of a detached console, in a gallery which had been built for it on the west wall of the College chapel. Much of the Laycock and Bannister work was later replaced by me and the organ further extended. The instrument now has a surprisingly comprehensive range of stops (including a cymbelstern) with a tonal spread far in excess of that originally envisaged by its first builder. It is in regular use for services and teaching.

ST MARY'S CATHOLIC CHURCH, DOUGLAS

Great: 8,8,8,8,4,4,2; Swell: 8,8,8,4,2,8,8; Pedal: 16,8.

The Catholic Church of St Mary of the Isle is one of the Island's most striking buildings and its impressive lofty interior results in one of the best acoustics to be found anywhere. Prominent in its spacious west gallery is the pipe organ which I restored in 2006. The instrument has been in its present home for almost 100 years. During the cleaning and restoration a message was discovered in a part of the mechanism rarely visible. Written in pencil by one of the organ builders who assembled the organ when it was brought to St Mary's from England it reads: 'November, 1913 This organ was brought from St Francis Xavier's College in Liverpool and erected in this church by Gray and Davison, Organ Builders, London and Liverpool. R.Johnson and A.Powell put up this organ. During the time we were here, there was an election of members of the House of Keys. 14.11.13.'

St Francis Xavier's College still exists but was moved from its original buildings in the 1960s. An organ was built there in 1885 as a memorial to a Father James Harris who was the Prefect of

Studies at the College. The stop list of that organ is basically the same as the organ in St Mary's today. The organ remained at the school for some 24 years, being taken out in 1909 and, with 2 additional stops and a new console it was moved to the Island and to St Mary's in 1913. By 2005 the instrument, though still working, was choked with dust and dirt, and its pipework was in a rather sorry state after at least 120 years service. The church authorities took the decision to commission a complete cleaning and overhaul. Every one of the 778 pipes was removed and individually cleaned and repaired, whilst the mechanism has also been cleaned and renovated. Many weeks were spent in the church, balancing the speech and volume of each pipe to fit its position within the overall sound of the organ, and the acoustics of the building. The result is an instrument which has one of the finest sounds of any on the Island, capable of leading the congregational singing and worthy of the church's dedicated choir.

CROSBY METHODIST CHAPEL

Manual: 8,8,4 Pedal: 16.

This is the smallest church organ on the Island in terms of numbers of stops. It was built by Forster and Andrews and is remarkably successful in this small chapel. All 3 manual stops are boldly voiced and enclosed in a swell-box, thus providing a wide range of power. The action is mechanical throughout. The names of former hand-blowers, pencilled onto the back of the swell-box, are notable in the small number of years shown for individuals holding this office, until one entry reveals that, 'W.Gladstone, M.P., visited this College on 1878.' from which it seems that part of the organ was once in King William's College, and the several organ-blowers of short duration were some of the boys.

ABBEYLANDS METHODIST CHAPEL

A reed-organ by Bell, of Canada.

These instruments were made by the hundreds of thousands in the late Victorian period and come in many shapes and sizes, intended for home and church use. The Abbeylands instrument was once in Derbyhaven Mission, where I completely overhauled it in 1984. It is notable for the impressive display of dummy wooden pipes and for its evocative tone, characteristic of this kind of instrument.

KIRK MICHAEL PARISH CHURCH

Great: 8,8,8,8,4,2; Swell: 8,8,4,2,8; Pedal: 16.

Built by Samuel Renn in 1852, this instrument was originally installed in Bishopscourt chapel in the 1850s, when it would have had 2 manuals and a set of 12 pedal pipes (instead of the present 30). Renn was a well-known builder in his day, and the bright, clear, quality of his pipework can still be appreciated. In 1878 the instrument was given to Kirk Michael Parish Church, at a time when Bevingtons (a London firm) supplied Bishopscourt with a much smaller 1-manual instrument. Presumably it was then that the organ was modernised and the further 18 pipes were added to the pedals.

PEEL METHODIST CHURCH

Great: 8,8,8,4,4,2; Swell: 16,8,8,8,4,8,8; Pedal: 16,16.

This 2-manual organ (built in 1892) is one of a pair by the firm of Alexander Young & Sons, the other being at Trinity United Reformed Church, Ramsey. The instrument has mechanical action to the manuals, and originally to the pedals, but the pedals were later converted to tubular pneumatic action. It is still possible to see the traces of gas lighting at the console, and the hand-blowing gear remains, though an electric blower has been in regular use for many years. Designed to accompany a full chapel of Methodist voices, the organ has a commanding presence, both visually and musically, thanks to its boldly-voiced main choruses, and excellent position at gallery level.

RUSHEN PARISH CHURCH

Great: 8,8,8,4,4; Swell: 16,8,8,8,8,4,2,8; Pedal: 16,16.

Built by Moses Morgan in 1904, this is his largest surviving instrument. It has 2 manuals and pedals, with mechanical action to the keys and stops, and pneumatic action to the 2 pedal stops. Excellently positioned in the west gallery the instrument projects its sound directly down the length of the building and is boldly voiced. The 16' violone pedal stop would be too tall to fit under the sloping gallery ceiling, were not the pipes ingeniously wrapped around themselves in such a way as to bring the mouths and the pipe tops down to almost the same level, and thereby halve the required standing room. The local moneyed family at the time in which the organ was installed were the Gawnes, who had a Morgan instrument in their music room at Kentraugh, later given to St Luke's, Baldwin, and they may have been a factor in commissioning this relatively large instrument from the local builder.

MAROWN PARISH CHURCH

Great: 8,8,8,8,8,4,4,2 2/3,2, 1 3/5, 8; Swell: 16,8,8,8,8,4,2,8,8; Pedal: 16,16.

This large, 2-manual organ was built by Alfred E Davies of Northampton and was originally in the Douglas Church of St Barnabas. Now sited in the north transept at Marown it is remarkable in its number of stops (the Great, for instance, has

what amounts to 3 diapasons) and complicated mechanical action to manuals, pedals and stops. This results in an instrument with a wide range of tone colours, but a heavy mechanism, though the organ speaks well into the building.

ST NINIAN'S CHURCH, DOUGLAS

Great: 8,8,8,8,4,4,2,8; Swell: 16,8,8,8,8,4,III,8,8, Pedal: 16,16,16,8.

This instrument was built by Norman and Beard in 1915 and was probably one of the very last to be built before they joined with William Hill and Sons after the First World War. Its construction is on a more massive scale than is found in many of the Island's organs, using heavy framing members, thick metal and timber for the pipework, 3 sets of bellows (the main ones being some of the largest found in any instrument) and a sensitive 3-stage pneumatic action, giving very good repetition of the notes.

The sound of the instruments is likewise massive, the overall effect being one of refined, smooth tones which are never shrill even at their loudest.

A spectacular pair of oak cases was planned in the gothic style (and these plans still exist) to clothe the organ in a way which would have matched the woodwork of this distinctive building, but these cases were never made, so the organ presents a rather austere front of grey zinc pipework on black timber support.

The bellows and pneumatic key actions have been re-leathered, and the console (which was originally up in the organ chamber) has been moved to floor level many years ago, but, other than this, the instrument remains exactly as the builders left it and is a tribute to Edwardian craftsmanship.

ST GEORGE'S CHURCH, DOUGLAS

Great: 8,8,4,4,2 2/3,2,IIII,8; Swell: 8,8,8,4,2,IIII,16,8,8; Pedal: 16,16,8,4,16.

The present organ was installed by Harrison and Harrison of Durham in 2003. It has a modern mechanical action to the manuals and pedals and direct electric stop action and piston action. The design at St George's is unusual, but not unique, in having the Swell section of the instrument sited above the Great. This allows the builders to have as much of the pipework as possible well forward in the case – a feature used to overcome the problem of a deep, narrow chamber. Its modern mechanical action, gleaming metal pipework, wooden pipes and components in polished, light-coloured timber make a stark contrast to the old instrument which had been there since the 1950s. The idea that the previous organ had some connection with Handel has often been mentioned, but this is unlikely. Although the 1950s organ incorporated parts of an older

Top Left: Rushen Parish Church.
Top Right: St George's Church, Douglas.
Middle: Marown Parish Church.
Above: St Ninian's Church, Douglas.
Right: St Paul's Church, Ramsey.

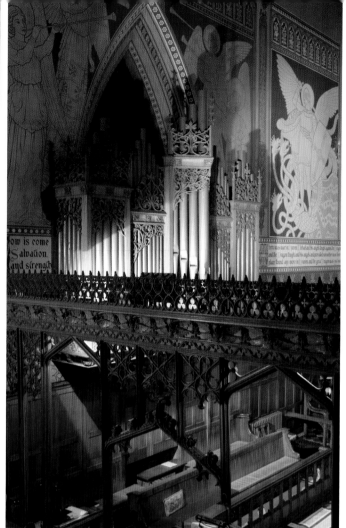

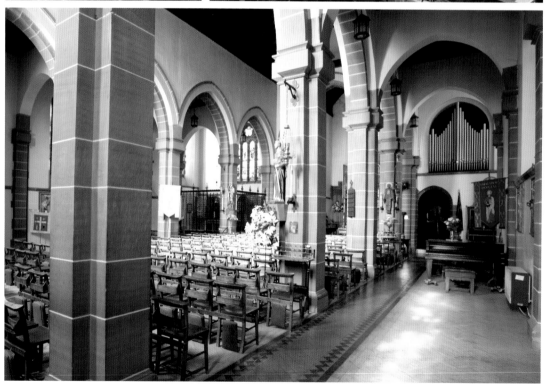

Top left: Trinity Methodist Church, Douglas.

Top Right: St Thomas's Church, Douglas.

Middle Left: Sulby Methodist Church.

Above: St Matthew's Church, Douglas.

instrument, the size of the soundboards and type of mechanism had nothing to do with the kind of organ which Handel would have known.

ST PAUL'S CHURCH, RAMSEY

Great: 8,8,8,8,4,4,2 2/3,2,8; Swell: 8,8,8,4,8,8; Pedal: 16,16.

This is a comprehensive 2-manual and pedal instrument, built by Forster and Andrews in 1883. It is sited in a wide, shallow chamber on the north wall. The pipework is generously scaled, with the pedal Bourdon stop the largest on the Island. The tone is smooth and refined, with a good selection of both loud and soft stops. The simple, pitch pine casework features a 'curtain' display of pipework, all of it colourfully patterned, and with the biggest pipe an over-sized dummy for a more impressive climax. The mechanism is decidedly heavy to play, as the pipe valves have been over-sized to ensure a sufficient wind supply.

ST THOMAS'S CHURCH, DOUGLAS

Great: 16,8,8,8,8,4,4,2 2/3,2,IIII,8; Swell: 16,8,8,8,8,4,2,III,16,8,8

Choir: 8,8,8,8,4; Pedal: (32),16,16,8.

One of only two 3-manual organs on the Island (the other being the reed-organ in Glen Maye Methodist Chapel) this is also the largest instrument in terms of numbers of pipes. Originally built by William Hill and Son as a 2-manual with mechanical action, it was rebuilt and enlarged by them following a fire in the tower and consequent water damage. It was reopened in 1913 as a 3-manual instrument with pneumatic action. The wind supply is provided by a truly impressive blowing plant, sited in a cellar under the organ, and a water-powered pump, which supplied the bellows before the advent of electricity, is still in its original position, though disconnected. Although repairs and cleaning have taken place down the years, the instrument remains much as Hills left it, with the smooth, refined tone for which the firm was noted, and what may be said to be the finest case of any organ on the Island.

TRINITY METHODIST CHURCH, DOUGLAS

Great: 8,8,8,8,4,4,2 2/3,2,III,8; Swell: 16,8,8,8,8,4,III 8,8; Pedal: 16,16.

One of our finest instruments, this is the largest of the Forster and Andrews organs found on the Island. Built in 1889 it has the solid, refined voicing found at St Paul's, Ramsey, and also, unfortunately, an equally heavy action! Whilst the sound is remarkable for its quality the casework of the instrument is little short of amazing – a true flight of Victorian fancy, in pitch pine

and multi-coloured display pipes. Excellently positioned on the front wall of the building it commands the eye from its site above the choir stalls, taking up virtually all of the available height.

SULBY METHODIST CHURCH

Manual: 8,8,4,4,2; Pedal: 16.

This 5-stop instrument started life as a chamber organ without pedals. It was modified to be more suitable as a church organ by Forster and Andrews, and installed in Sulby in February 1887. They added sections to the casework and provided the appropriate mechanism to accommodate a set of pedal pipes on each side of the player. They also enlarged the scaling (the relative size of the pipes) in several of the stops with a view to making the instrument louder, and it is likely that they added the swell-box. The dignified, veneered case, with its dummy wooden display pipes and inlaid woods around the keyboard is typical of an 18th century chamber organ, and the tone is sweet and mellow. The hand-blowing gear is still in place, and written on some of the less accessible parts of the case and pipes are some of the names of former blowers, including the possibly unique inscription in memory of a Mr Kneale, who died 'hanging from a tree', in the early 1900s.

ST MATTHEW'S CHURCH, DOUGLAS

Great: 16,8,8,8,4,4,2 2/3,2,II,8,8,4; Swell: 8,8,8,8,4,2,III,16,8; Pedal: 16,16,8,8,4,2.

This comprehensive 2-manual and pedal instrument is a favourite with visiting recitalists. Originally built in the 1920s by Earnest Wadsworth of Manchester, it had a detached console and tubular pneumatic action. When this became unreliable in the 1970s it was decided to turn to an electronic instrument. The console was destroyed, but, fortunately, the organ itself was left in situ. When the electronic eventually failed, the pipe organ was renovated by Philip Wood of Huddersfield, who provided it with an electro-pneumatic action and a new console. The stop list was also revised. In recent years I have added further stops, including the Pedal Trombone, to make this instrument, with its wide selection of tone colours and comfortable, modern console, one of the most versatile organs on the Island.

For photographs and a fuller account of these and other church and chapel organs on the Island, visit the Manx Heritage Foundation's website at www.manxheritage.org/organs

GLOSSARY

Aisle – (1) a central passageway through a church (what the bride walks down) (2) a stone or brick lean-to on the north or south side of a church, providing more space.

Altar –a stone chest or wooden table in the sanctuary, at which the minister celebrates Communion. In the Church of England and by Nonconformists properly called a holy table.

Altar-rails – low wooden or metal railings separating the sanctuary from the rest of the church, originally to keep dogs out but now used to kneel at to receive Communion.

Anglican – a member of the Church of England.

Anglo-Catholic – an Anglican who also sees himself as a catholic; services are closer to Roman Catholic practice than in the mainstream Church of England, and often include incense and elaborate robes

Arcade – a row of arches.

Archdeacon – a senior clergyman whose duties include enforcing Church rules, especially in relation to church buildings.

Art Nouveau – artistic style c 1890 - c 1910, all sinuous curves.

Arts and Crafts – architectural movement c 1890- c 1920, inspired by traditional cottages and craftsmanship.

Baptism – Christening – immersing or pouring water on a baby in a font to make him a member of the Church; traditional doctrine said only the baptised could go to Heaven.

Baptist – member of a Nonconformist denomination believing baptism should take place not in infancy but in adulthood when it is a conscious decision by the baptised.

Baptistry – part of a church containing a font; generally a catholic term.

Baron – a high rank in the feudal hierarchy in the Middle Ages and later; in the Isle of Man came directly under the King.

Bellcote – a small open-air stone frame at the top of the west end of a church, containing one or two bells rung to mark services.

Bell-turret – miniature tower at the west end of a church, containing one or two bells.

Bishop – the senior clergyman in charge of a diocese.

Box Pews – seats in a church within a rectangular or square enclosure of low wooden partitions, one or all of which form the backs of the seats; the partitions extend all round to include a door.

Cathedral – the principal church of a diocese.

Cemetery – a churchyard without a church (except one used only for funerals).

Chancel – the east part of a church, containing the sanctuary.

Church Rates – a tax formerly paid by all owners or occupiers of houses or land and used for various local government purposes by the minister and churchwardens, under the control of the Vestry.

Churchwardens – in the Church of England, laymen supervising the maintenance of the church and churchyard, and historically much else in the parish besides; in the seventeen ancient parishes in the Isle of Man, four or six in number, elected by the people; in other parishes, two, one appointed by the minister and one elected by the congregation.

Classical – architectural style based on that of ancient Greece and Rome.

Communion – church service involving distribution to the congregation of bread and wine, in memory of Christ's Last Supper.

Consecration – ceremony by a bishop setting apart a building or land for religious purposes.

Crossing – the centre of a cruciform church.

Cruciform – cross-shaped, the commonest plan for a Gothic church.

Crypt – basement or cellar of a church.

Cupola – miniature dome.

Desk – where a minister sits, kneels or stands to take a church service.

Diocese – area of church administration consisting of a number of parishes, usually about the size of an English county.

Doric – one of the simplest types of classical column.

Ecclesiologists – a very successful pressure group in the Church of England from the 1840's, wanting the design and

Above: St Patrick's Isle, the greatest of Manx religious sites, with on the left the Round Tower and on the right the Cathedral, both now within the walls of Peel Castle.

arrangement of churches to be altered to what they thought mediaeval churches had been like. They were generally also members of the Oxford Movement.

Elim Pentecostal – a Nonconformist denomination of the 20th and 21st centuries, having extrovert services.

Encaustic tiles – glazed tiles used on the floors of some mediaeval churches, revived in a mass-produced form in Victorian times.

Episcopate – period when someone is a bishop.

Eucharist – Greek word for Communion, fashionable among late 20th century modernisers.

Fluted – (of a column) with shallow vertical grooves, like corrugated cardboard.

Font – large basin (usually stone) on a pedestal; filled with water for baptisms.

Friary – a home for itinerant monks called friars, often followers of St Francis of Assisi.

Frontal – embroidered cloth covering the front of altars; largely unknown between the Reformation and the nineteenth century, for a time nearly universal but now going out of favour with the popularity of freestanding nave altars.

Gothic – architectural style used for most churches from c 1200 to the seventeenth century, and again from the early nineteenth century to the early twentieth; characterised by pointed windows and pointed arches.

Gothick – minority architectural style of the later eighteenth

and early 19th centuries, a lighter, more playful form of Gothic.

High Church – that element in the Church of England favouring Anglo-Catholic practice.

Label – a small moulding above a window, decorative but also casting off the rain.

Lancet- a narrow, pointed window.

Lantern – an octagonal or hexagonal drum-shaped structure with windows on top of a tower or roof.

Layman – anyone not a clergyman.

Lectern – a type of easel (often in the shape of an eagle) on which is kept a bible used for reading lessons in church services; introduced into most churches by the ecclesiologists.

Ledgerstone – a rectangular stone, about 6' x 3', covering a burial in the aisle of a church or in a churchyard, with an inscription containing the name of the deceased; common in the seventeenth and eighteenth centuries.

Liturgy – a set form of worship; the traditional liturgy of the Church of England is the Prayer Book.

Low Church – that element in the Church of England which was largely dominant before the Oxford Movement in the 1840's and which has simpler services and is unambiguously Protestant not catholic.

Lychgate – roofed gateway to a churchyard.

Manse - residence of a Nonconformist minister.

Mass – Roman Catholic and Anglo-Catholic name for Communion; unlike Protestants, they believe the bread and wine actually turn into Christ's body and blood.

Methodist – member of a group founded by an Anglican minister John Wesley in the eighteenth century and which subsequently became a separate church; a Low Church Anglicanism without bishops.

Minister – a clergyman of the Church of England and other Protestant churches.

Modern – architectural style of the mid-twentieth century, emphasising clean lines and modern materials.

Mortar – a large bowl (often stone) used for grinding with a pestle.

Mothers' Union – Anglican women's organisation.

Mullion – a vertical bar dividing a window.

Nave – the largest part of most churches, extending to the west end; where most of the congregation sit.

Nonconformist – someone who does not conform to the Church of England; Methodists, Presbyterians, Baptists, etc.

North, south, east, west – in most traditional churches, the altar is at the east and the main entrance at the west; even if the church is not actually so aligned, its parts are often described as though it was, sometimes refined as 'liturgical east', etc.

Oxford Movement – High Church movement in the Church of England from the 1840's; many of its members eventually became Roman Catholics.

Parish – the whole country is divided into parishes (of the Church of England), each with its own church and a minister designated to look after it; up until the nineteenth century also the main unit of local government.

Parish Church – the principal church of a parish.

Parish Clerk – layman who led the congregation in their responses in Anglican services, and helped keep up the registers etc; in the Isle of Man traditionally elected by the people.

Parson – traditional colloquial name for an Anglican minister.

Pediment – the low triangular top element of many classical buildings.

Perpendicular – the latest phase of Gothic architecture (the others are Early English and Decorated); often lighter and less massive.

Pilaster – flat column applied to the surface of a classical building.

Piscina – small recess in mediaeval church used for washing sacred vessels; often with a decorative arched top.

Popish – veering towards Roman Catholicism; an uncomplimentary term.

Prayer Book – the Book of Common Prayer, put into its final form in 1662, is the traditional (and officially still the principal) liturgy of the Church of England (and used with very little modification by traditional Methodists).

Presbyterian – a Protestant denomination, characterised by not having bishops; the established church in Scotland.

Presbytery – residence of a Roman Catholic priest.

Priest – Roman Catholic clergyman (also used by Anglo-Catholics).

Pro-cathedral – a temporary or acting cathedral.

Protestant – those who left the Roman Catholic church at the Reformation, including Anglicans and Nonconformists (although Anglo-Catholics reject the label).

Pulpit – raised box in which a minister stands to preach.

Purgatory – in Roman Catholic doctrine, somewhere the soul goes between death and Heaven, a journey which may be expedited by prayers of the living; a concept rejected by Protestants.

Quakers – a Nonconformist denomination characterised by great simplicity of their services and (traditionally) of their dress.

Quoins – large square stones all up the outside corners of a building.

Reformation – in the sixteenth century, when many especially in northern Europe left the Roman Catholic church and corrected what they saw as its errors, becoming Protestants.

Ritualist – a name given to Anglo-Catholics, because of their love of ritual in worship.

Romanesque – style of architecture (in the British Isles used for most churches from 1000 to 1200) characterised by round arches (like those used by the Romans, hence the name).

Rood Screen – screen of wood or stone between nave and chancel, so called because before the Reformation it was topped with a rood (a figure of Christ on the cross).

Sanctuary – the very easternmost part of a church, containing the altar.

Squarson – someone who is simultaneously squire and parson.

Stalls – seats in a church facing inwards, used by ministers or a choir; generally a Victorian introduction.

Sunday School – where children are given religious instruction, often at the same time as or before or after a church service.

Tracery – ornamental stonework dividing the upper part of a Gothic pointed window into separate panes.

Transept – the north and south projections of a cruciform church, usually roughly square in shape; used for extra seating.

Venetian window – in classical architecture a window of three lights, the outer two vertical and rectangular, the centre with a rounded top rising higher than the others.

Vestry – (1) the assembly of ratepayers which governed a parish until it lost most of its powers in the later nineteenth century (2) a small room in a church where the minister dresses for the service, often also used for storage, a safe, etc.

Winged soul – a device found on some more primitive gravestones of the seventeenth and eighteenth centuries consisting of a stylised face with wings, the exact significance a subject of some dispute.